Copyright © 2025 by Julie Monks

All rights reserved.

No part of this book may be reproduced in any form, by photocopying or by any electronic or mechanical means, including information storage or retrieval systems, without permission in writing from the copyright owner.

ISBN – 9798345721544

Illustrations by Ian Lloyd

Edited by and published in collaboration with Penny Thresher at Corner House Words

https://cornerhousewords.co.uk

Contents

	V
Introduction	1
How to read this book	5
1. Find your Mentors	7
2. Taking Action	15
3. Activate your RAS	33
4. Did you say what I think you said?	57
5. The Business of Work	79
6. Money	104
7. Compassion over Comparison	125
8. Dealing With Overwhelm	137
9. Resilience to Brilliance	154
10. Rule Book Roulette	174
Epilogue	185
Reading List	187

For Dave, my husband, who supported me emotionally and financially during the writing process.

...and who also provides me with an endless supply of material for my stories.

Introduction

30th October 2020.

Many of the people I have coached over the years have assumed that I would write a book one day. I have been procrastinating about this for a long time.

Over the last 10 years, I made a lot of notes and even completed a few chapters, but somehow something always got in the way. Too many distractions and I always seemed too busy with work.

But here I am, in lockdown, smack bang in the middle of a pandemic, writing this introduction! For the time being, I cannot blame being busy for my lack of progress.

Another big reason for not writing my book has been my fear of ridicule. Who the hell would be interested in anything I have to say? Who am I to tell others how to live their lives?

Yet in conversation, people often tell me that after spending time with me, they always come away feeling energised. And many of them have made significant life-changing decisions after my coaching sessions.

Currently, I would say that I am 'not working.' At least I am not 'employed.' But I am a company director and an administrator for two companies. My father-in-law's, and the one my husband and I own.

So why write a book now?

Well, my motto is 'Shit or bust!'

I recently signed up to a program run by one of my mentors, the amazing Shelley Booth. This has involved a lot of work on myself, both physically and mentally, leading to a reassessment of many things in my life.

Until now, I have watched other people doing the things I thought I might do, and whilst congratulating them and celebrating their success, I have had a nagging feeling inside me that it should have been me!

I follow the teachings of Abraham Hicks, and I read many personal development books. Everything I have learned has finally convinced me to just write the damn book anyway, and not to give a damn whether anybody reads it or criticises it!

There is still that little voice inside me, telling me that no one would have anything good to say about it. But for once, I am not listening. Funnily enough, I was listening to an Abraham Hicks podcast recently and the message to me was loud and clear.

'JUST WRITE THE BOOK'

If nothing else, I will write it for my children and grandchildren, so I can pass my wisdom on to them.

I was always a bossy child, and I loved telling everyone what to do. The best school report I ever had was when I was 7 years old.

'Julie is very good at talking,' it read. Nothing changes!

Mine is not exactly a 'rags to riches' story. More like 'slightly tatty clothes to the top end of the high street' one.

But I believe I can help people lead happier and more fulfilling lives by offering advice based on everything that I have learned over the years, either from experience or research. This is driving me to write this book now. I feel sad when I see so many people who never reach their full potential.

This book is not about becoming a millionaire, although that is not a bad goal to aim for. It is about becoming the best you can be.

We all have something significant to say in this world; a part to play. I do not believe that our path is pre-determined. We can change our direction at any time. The first step is the first step; wanting to change and acting on that desire.

One of my favourite sayings is:

'Take my advice. I'm not using it.'

I have noticed that people often ask for advice but are not genuinely looking for someone to guide them. What they want is someone to agree with a decision they have already made.

The funny thing is, we often know what we need to do to improve our lives or situation, but for some unknown reason, we fear taking the necessary action; me included.

15th July 2024

Well, that took a little longer that I expected. A thought popped into my head, 'If I had known 4 years ago what I know now, I am sure that I would have tackled writing this book differently'.

It has been an enlightening experience! There have been times of inspiration, where the words have just flown from my head faster that I could type them. But also, times where I have felt like abandoning it completely.

Ironically, I lost count of how many times I needed to take my own advice!

My intention, when I started writing this book, was to help you discover some ways to make your life a little smoother by sharing the lessons I've learned the hard way.

If this book can bring about any improvement in your life, no matter how small, then I consider my mission accomplished.

Enjoy x

Julie

How to read this book

Get the best out of every page

I love reading and always have a personal development book on the go.

Some of them I read straight through, take in the information I need, but rarely return to.

I also have a few that I keep in a handy place as reference books and constantly return to them as I use them as a guide depending on what my current needs are.

A few of my constant companion books are

The Magic - *Rhonda Byrne* - gives me a new exercise for each day.

Eat That Frog! - *Brian Tracy* - when I need motivation

Who Moved My Cheese? – *Spencer Johnson* – when I am facing a change in circumstances

Energy Alignment Method - *Yvette Taylor* - helps me to regulate my feelings

There are many more of my favourite books referred to throughout this one; you can find full details in the Reading List at the back of the book.

I have designed this book as an easy reading life manual that you can choose to read in one hit; or one you can pick up and cherry pick whichever bit of information you need, when you need it!

I like to think of it as a recipe book; something you pick up when you need help or inspiration.

It is an easy read, a light-hearted handbook for life full of tips, advice and personal stories which I hope readers can relate to. For people who are just starting their journey with personal development books, but also for people like me who seeking new inspiration.

Chapter One

Find your Mentors

Choose the people that influence you wisely

> *'You are the average of the 5 people you surround yourself with.'* - Jim Rohn

Imagine a mentor as your personal Yoda, but hopefully with better fashion sense!

Like a wise, old video game character who dispenses knowledge, helps you level up your skills, and guides you on your epic quest, which could be anything from conquering public speaking to mastering that tricky recipe. A mentor is your personal cheerleader, your walking advice column, and your real-life cheat code for navigating life's adventures. They have been there, done that, and have the battle scars and funny anecdotes to prove it. Basically, they are there to help you become the awesome hero of your own story!

Who influences you?

Never underestimate the influence of those around you. No matter how positive your mindset is, we are all subconsciously affected by the people we spend the most time with.

Without realising it, we take on little habits, good and bad, from people around us. We absorb their energy too. If I am spending time with a friend who is into her fitness and health, then I am more likely to be attending regular gym sessions and eating healthy food. Whereas, when I spend time with friends who overeat and don't exercise, it is easy for me to slip into those bad habits.

Find your people

- Who are the people that leave you feeling energised and happy, maybe even on a bit of a high, when you spend time or hold a conversation with them?

- Who are the people that are a good influence on you?

- Who are the friends that support and encourage you in all your ventures?

- Who are the friends that always look for the good in you and compliment you?

- Who are the friends that will always give you an honest opinion in the kindest way possible?

- Who are the friends that inspire you to be more like them?

- Who are the people you admire and look up to?

- Who do you know that has achieved something that you aspire to?

These are your people.

The people you should spend most of your time with. The people that leave you feeling great about yourself.

Over the last 40 years, I have encountered many wonderful people who have mentored me and made a positive difference in my life. They have encouraged me to believe in myself and guided me along a better and more fulfilling path. I would like to thank every one of them for the massive impact they have made in my life. This book is my way of giving back; sharing the advice and lessons that have benefited me. I realise that not everyone is as lucky as me to find such people.

Let me be one of *your* mentors

My father lost his job frequently. Mainly because he did not like being told what to do and then, in later life, through ill health. He had an inferiority complex; something that is not mentioned these days but is still alive and kicking. Although it is now referred to as 'mental health' or 'anxiety issues.'

I passionately believe that if he had followed a path of self-development study and listened to the right mentors, he would have set up and run a successful business. He attempted to do so in the past but failed. According to him, it was always someone else's fault.

He had a persecution complex too. Being employed did not suit his personality, but he simply did not have enough self-belief to push forward and take the risks needed to run his own business. He even had business cards printed for an Import/Export business called Ankara Agency, but never took it any further. He spent the last 20 years of his life in a wheelchair, staring out of the window, full of bitterness and regret; all of which I am sure translated into his poor health.

My father's inferiority complex heavily influenced me when I was younger. I felt I did not measure up to my peers, whether at school or in the working environment. I can see now that this turned out to be an asset, as it pushed me to build a better life for myself and my children.

> *Even as I am writing this book, I am expecting criticism. Is this normal? Does everyone feel this way?*
> *– Julie*

At school, I struggled to read. I had poor eyesight and I am sure this put me at a disadvantage. Even as a child, I was aware there was a better way to live. I became someone who wanted to impress others.

Despite their general discouragement, my parents pushed me towards academia and fully expected that I would attend university. My mother even chose my options for me at age 13. She was a very academic lady; a member of Mensa and she studied for an Open University degree in her late sixties. The thing they overlooked was that I was a practical person who found it hard to concentrate in the classroom and could not apply myself to studying or revising.

I frequently felt frustrated when doing my homework. I remember believing I would suddenly pull it out of the bag and a miracle would happen so that I could attend Uni and become a bilingual secretary in my last year of high school. A career that was not even on my radar! It was my parent's expectation. As an only child, my parents pinned all their hopes and dreams on me.

By this time, I had one year left with no prospect of passing my exams. Nor had I come up with an alternate career plan. This was 1977 and unemployment was at an all-time high.

By chance, the position of Saturday girl became vacant in the local hairdressing salon. Looking back now, I see that this was an early brush with the Law of Attraction. I took the job purely to earn some cash. With my father invalided out of work, money was tight in our household.

I never wanted to be a hairdresser. As a child, when my friends talked about what they wanted to be, an air hostess, a model, or a hairdresser, I had no such ambition. For a 15-year-old girl, I was very rough around the edges and a bit of a tomboy. I had no clue about personal care, and I certainly had zero self-confidence.

It turned out that this job was the best thing that could have happened to me. I am still grateful for that opportunity. It changed the course of my life for the better, thanks to the three ladies who took me under their wings and mentored me. Back then, I didn't realise that was what they were doing, but massive thanks to Carol, Liz, and Yvonne. I owe you so much and will always be grateful to you all.

So, what did they do that was so life changing for me?

First, I discovered I was very good at washing hair and the clients loved the firmness of my hands. These ladies praised and encouraged me and for the first time since I gave up gymnastics aged 12, I believed I was good at something. They treated me like an adult, listened to my problems, and gave me brilliant advice. Under their mentorship, my confidence grew.

Liz took me aside and taught me to look after my skin, telling me I would thank her for it one day. Aged 62 I still have amazing skin; she gave me sound advice. They taught me how to dress and look after myself, encouraging me to pursue hairdressing as a career. Liz even came with me to my first job interview. Carol was like a mother hen. Yvonne was the trendy one who had worked for Vidal Sassoon in the swinging 60s. They all had interesting stories to tell, and they would often link them to sound advice.

Be aware of your external influences

'I attended the University of Life'

How many times have you heard someone say that, or read it on their social media profiles?

It is something I genuinely believe applies to me. I am aware it means very different things to each person. To me, it means seeing every day as a chance to learn a new lesson.

Not everyone has access to great people in their lives, but never underestimate the power of other forms of outside influence. It is not only the people around us that influence us. What we read, what we watch, and everything we see on social media also has an effect.

We cannot hide away in a cave and avoid what is going on in the bigger world around us, but we can choose what we focus on. Personally, I know that if I spend too much time watching rubbish TV, or listening to the news and reading the newspapers, it affects my mood and my productivity in an extremely negative way. We need to look for positive influences that raise our vibration and energise us.

All the self-development books I have read have contributed to my quest to improve my life skills, and I have discovered many of the people I have chosen as mentors in those pages. With the wealth of audio books and podcasts now available, there is an endless supply of educational, inspirational material in easy reach for all of us. I hope that through this book and my coaching practice, I will become part of your personal growth journey.

TAKE MY ADVICE

Spend most of your time with the people that lift your vibration and energise you

Limit your time with toxic and draining people

Look for mentors in books and podcasts

Only take advice from people who have achieved what you aspire to

---

Who are *your* mentors?

If you don't have any, who would you choose to connect with?

Chapter Two

Taking Action

You can change your default setting - I am proof of that.

J ust because you have always behaved in a certain way; or you keep making the same mistakes repeatedly, does not mean that you are stuck in this mode.

- 'I am disorganised.'
- 'I am always late.'
- 'I have never been good with my hands.'

These are just some things I often hear people say.

Well, I have some great news for you. None of this is set in stone.

You (yes, I mean YOU!) are capable of anything - if you want it enough.

These limiting beliefs become ingrained in us from our experiences or the environment we grew up in. Or from something someone said to us in the past.

No matter where the beliefs come from, they become hard-wired in our brains, and we simply do not believe we can control or change certain behaviours.

'Oh! Just give me the jumper and get on with it'

I watched an interview with Joanna Lumley, and she told a story about when she was a fledgling actor. She used to model for knitting patterns. Even after she was famous, her agent would still get requests for her to model knitwear. Intent on turning the jobs down, her agent would state brusquely, 'Ms Lumley no longer does this kind of work'.

But Joanna would step in. 'Oh...just give me the jumper,' she would say.

For me, that story has become a metaphor for 'Just stop thinking about it and get on with it. Once it's done, it's done; I don't have to waste any more time letting that task take up space in my head.'

Oh, the lists are endless!

Some people love lists, while others hate them. A list helps some people feel in control; others fear the sense of failure that not achieving everything on their list will bring them.

Personally, I love a list! It gives my day structure. Over the years, I have discovered some helpful ways to deal with the tackling of tasks.

Attending a Franklin Covey 'What Matters Most' course in 1999 was a complete game changer for me and everyone else who attended. Ever since then, I have used their time management system.

The DAN task list

My DAN task list has evolved as a simplified way of putting into practice what I learned all those years ago. This method will improve your relationship with lists.

D – Deadline of the day

- Does it need to be done today?
- If we don't do it today, will it be too late?

A nice and easy example for this is bin collection day. If you don't get your bins out in time, the task of bin collection loses value, as it cannot be completed within the time frame.

D tasks are often things that have arisen during the day and need to be executed instantly. If you are not in control and not great at forward preparation, then D tasks become last minute firefighting undertakings. My D list would include all those head fizzle jobs!

The ideal scenario is to only have a few D tasks on your list. Some of us excel under pressure and thrive on working right up to the wire. But this can be incredibly stressful for most people and will have a negative impact on your wellbeing.

A – Ahead preparation; Important, not yet urgent tasks

These are mainly deadline driven tasks too, but usually for a future deadline as opposed to one that needs to be completed that day.

This is where we can be most productive. In the long term, this will help you create a better balance in your life and work. Things will flow more easily.

This is all about forward planning; preparing for meetings; dealing with important emails; getting things done in advance so that there is no rush when a deadline looms, ruling out last-minute disasters.

Extremely useful when faced with complicated jobs, or jobs that you dislike. For example, submitting your annual tax return.

My personal favourite is the VAT Return. I always used to leave it until the last minute, which meant that occasionally I would miss the deadline and receive a £100 fine. Nowadays, it is a lot simpler. We have accounting software that does all the calculations for us. Of course, we still need to enter all the data first!

Now I aim to have the return completed 15 days before the deadline, and I spend a small amount of time each day entering the transactions as they arise.

This only takes a few minutes and is quite enjoyable when there is no pressure. I also have time to spot and correct errors. Even routine, boring tasks such as doing the monthly bank reconciliation become simple when I enter all the information.

This section is the one where you should spend the most time. It will be the most productive too.

N - Nice

Nice tasks are non-urgent. Things that you enjoy doing.

Most people find it easier to work with some structure in their day. Lists work well within that structure. But it is all too easy to cherry pick the pleasant tasks on your list rather than dealing with the more important stuff. When you do this, you will find there are still important items left on your list that need attention, leaving you feeling you have accomplished nothing.

When I worked in social selling, I had many conversations with my team members who would express how busy they were, looking after and managing their own team. And complaining that they did not have time to make the sales and recruitment calls needed to keep their own businesses afloat. They were in headless chicken mode.

I too have been guilty of this, focusing and prioritising the 'nice-to-do,' rather than dealing with the jobs I did not enjoy, or even dreaded.

If this happens, your N-tasks could become your D-tasks of the future.

N Tasks are the things that could be done when you find yourself with a little extra time once you have completed your D and A-tasks. Alternatively, you could fit them in while waiting for a callback or have a cancellation. If completed, they are a bonus.

Once you have mastered this method, the items on your list will be mainly As and Ns. Any outstanding D-tasks will be a consequence of something that occurred during that day or a regular task that you must complete on a set day of the week.

Make it colourful

I love to make notes of conversations and meetings, even though I often I frequently struggle to read my own writing!

Sitting in meetings and conferences that lasted for days, I found it useful to write action points at the end of each section. Later, I would struggle to find the notes relevant to the action points I needed to address.

Paper notes work best for me; you must use what is best for you. Using different coloured pens has become a simple way to help me follow up and keep on track.

Black or blue pen - Basic notes

Green pen - My action points

Red pen - Action points for the other person, if we are in a one-to-one conversation, or for the company if in a business meeting.

Purple pen – Team action points

Simple but effective.

Give it 100% attention - Is multi-tasking a myth?

Don't get me wrong, there is a place for multi-tasking. But in this world of constant notifications from emails, What's App and social media, it can be tempting to react immediately to the constant interruptions. Years ago, my friend Carolyn Passey gave me a brilliant piece of advice. 'Where possible, focus on one job at a time and give it 100% whilst you are doing it.'

Hmm I have just picked up my phone as I am writing this sentence. Yet another example of take my advice; I am not using it! – Julie

Carolyn gave me an example; when she was bathing her children after a long day at work, she would focus 100% on bath and story time and not let anything distract her from her time with her kids.

This advice has been invaluable. When you focus on the now, without jumping ahead to the next thing on your list, you will learn to fully enjoy whichever activity you immerse yourself in. This will lead to less stress and a less anxious mind.

Take My Advice

Make family mealtimes a priority

Ban all screens from the table

Switch your phone to Do Not Disturb mode when you are busy with another task

Only access your emails when you intend to deal with them

Limit yourself to dealing with email at set times of the day

Unless you are required to be on call 24/7, switch your computer off once your working day has finished. The best way to ruin a great night's sleep is to check your mailbox at bedtime!

I remember one of my team members bemoaning the fact that her team would call her at any time of the day. Even at 11pm!

'Do you answer your phone?' I asked.

'Yes,' she replied.

There is the answer. If you make yourself available all the time, then you set the expectation that you are available all the time. Setting and communicating your working hours is important.

Social media is another enormous distraction but has become an integral part of our working life. Especially important if you are self-employed. Take a quick peek at the screen time app on your phone. I guarantee you will be shocked by the time you spend scrolling on social media. Full disclosure – I was guilty of this until recently.

While it is lovely to see what your long-lost school friends are up to, it is too easy to get caught up. Before you know it, several hours have passed. This is not productive, and we often become so immersed that we are not present in our own lives.

When I see parents of young children pushing their strollers, but looking at their phones, ignoring their children, I feel so sad. Time flies and is precious. What a waste, to miss out on our own lives while wasting time immersed in the cyber life of others.

Multi-tasking is a myth. Of course, it is possible to do multiple things at once. We do it naturally all the time. We walk and talk without thinking about it - our subconscious minds deal with it for us.

But when you are doing two things simultaneously, you are only dedicating 50% of your attention to each task. So, the result can only ever be worth 50%.

Never put off until tomorrow what you can do today

Oh, how I wished I had learned this years ago.

I grew up with parents who were more 'never do today, what you can put off forever'. They would leave all the small things left undone until they became HUGE! My mother's to do list book had written on the cover. 'The road to hell is paved with good intentions.'

For years, I followed my parent's blueprint. I found myself completely overwhelmed by simple things, such as admin and household tasks.

Feeling overwhelmed; wasting time – minutes, hours, days, weeks, years; thinking about the things I should have done or needed to get done. Feeling like even the most mundane of tasks was too big a mountain to climb. I became expert at finding excuses or creating diversions.

For example, 5 years of bookkeeping I had not touched. I thought about it every day, but still did nothing about it. Your mind does not know the difference between doing it and thinking about it. No wonder I felt exhausted all the time.

My other big thing was my house. I have owned a house since I was 21. As I am writing this book, that amounts to 39 years of ownership. It took me until I was in my mid-50s to learn the art of keeping my house in good order with relative ease.

Of course, I could simply have paid a cleaner, and I did that for years.

If it is within your budget, I would totally advocate getting a cleaner. If you hate doing housework; if you run your own business; if you have a busy job – all good reasons, and there are many more.

If you have staff to cater to your every whim, you are probably not reading this book. But for those of you that are, here is another bit of invaluable advice, given to me by my good friend Gill Golding when I was in my early 50s.

Organic Organisation

Do it when you see it. For example, if you spill something, just mop it up. You do not need to clean the entire area.

There are plenty of experts sharing plans and theories that say that you need to have the BIG sort out and clear out. I agree this is sometimes necessary, but it's not always possible to be in that mindset. Sometimes it is too big a mountain to climb.

You may be familiar with the phrase, 'Every journey begins with the first step.' You can apply this to tidying and sorting. Start by moving just one thing that is out of place or needs to be discarded. If you are feeling brave, start with one small area, preferably the one that is bothering you the most.

Lots of tidying gurus suggest you start with a drawer or a cupboard. That's great, but the disadvantage of this approach is that you will only see it when you open it, whereas if you clean a space that you see all the time, you will feel the benefit constantly.

My friend used to joke with me about the fact that the insides of all my kitchen cupboards were in perfect order, but all the bits you could see were a total mess.

'You've got it the wrong way round, Julie.' She would say.

The truth of the matter is that, for most of us, being surrounded by clutter and unfinished jobs is incredibly stressful and very energy draining. Eventually, this may even lead to mental health problems.

If none of this helps, and you are still feeling overwhelmed, I recommend getting the experts in. Get some help.

But here are my suggestions to get you started:

- Never walk past something that is in the wrong place unless you have your hands full.

- If it is in a cupboard or a drawer and it is not visible, it is not a priority.

- Start by dealing with the stuff you can see and is annoying you or creating obstacles around the house.

- If you work from home, start with your office or workspace. If you do not have enough time for the whole area, start with your desk. Tackle it one pile at a time.

- If you have time, sort your documents into three piles using the DAN task list.

- Shred, recycle, file and complete paperwork as you sort through.

- Discard any unnecessary clutter as you go.

- Decide if you need an item to be nearby and put it out of sight if you don't.

- I keep my diary, pens, and notebook to hand and I store most of my stuff in my desk drawer, organised in easy-to-reach sections. The aim is to have as little as possible distracting you when you are working. Once you have achieved this, make a point of clearing it at the end of every working day.

> *Looking at my desk right now, it really is a case of, take my advice; I'm not using it!* – Julie

Once all that is complete, clear the rest of the room – this might be when you need to clear a cupboard or drawer to make space.

Be ruthless! If you have not used an item, ask yourself:

- Why am I holding on to this?

- Is it of sentimental value or is it useful? If so, how likely am I to use it?

- Can I live without it?

- Is it in your way?

- How do you feel just looking at it?

- Is it a good feeling? Check out the Marie Kondo method. Does it spark joy? A useful strategy to use in this instance.

Once your workspace is clear, start on the next room or task that is bugging you the most.

For example: that pile of ironing – think about how you will feel when you have cleared it. If you don't have time to tackle the full job right now, allocate a time slot for it.

Even if you can dedicate one hour a day to clearing and sorting, you will be surprised how quickly you can gain control of your surroundings.

When I find myself in any situation where there seem to be several muddles accumulating around the house, the solution is to have what I call a quick stealth session. This could be just an hour. Or, if it is bad, I will allocate a whole day.

I go round the house, visiting every room, and giving each one a re-set. It is a brilliant way of getting yourself out of a slump. And you will reclaim the time spent by being more productive once it is done.

Creating Good Habits

Put things back in their place as you go, rather than leaving it until it becomes an enormous task again.

Ideally, reset each room once you have finished with it for the day. Then you can start the next day feeling unfettered. A cluttered living space causes a cluttered mind.

This has worked very well for me over the last two years. I spend less time on housework, yet my house always looks clean and tidy. Another plus to this is that I am happy to receive unexpected visitors, as there is no need for me to rush madly around the house, shoving things into cupboards or under beds if a visit is imminent. I feel more at peace in my home and can relax.

Measured mantra

I am one of those all-or-nothing people; thinking I must be 'in the zone' to perform. I am also an impatient person. I have made mistakes in the past, big and small, because of this attitude.

When observing other people, I have noticed that those who accomplish a lot in a small amount of time never give the impression they are rushing around or feeling harassed. Deciding this is a much better way forward and fighting my natural tendency to rush, I begin by chanting in my head.

'Slow and steady wins the prize.'

Of course, you will sometimes find yourself in a dangerous situation and you need to react quickly. But a slow, measured approach to most tasks will bring you better results with less stress.

We must discover our best way of living without making excuses, to ourselves or others.

DID IT List

Every day is different.

Instead of writing yet another to do list, jot down all the things that you have done, saying 'I did it!' out loud after each one. Maybe just whisper it to yourself if you are in a public place!

This will help with feelings of guilt if you are lacking in focus or cannot find the energy to perform that part of the day.

Just this morning, I woke up feeling lethargic. I simply wanted to sit and read a novel, despite knowing that I had 504 words to write before my meeting at 11 am with Penny, my lovely, supportive writing coach.

Sitting on the step, staring into space, I made a mental list of all the jobs I had completed over the weekend. The list was long and included some very arduous tasks. Reviewing everything I had accomplished helped me to understand that I was exhausted. My body needed rest, so I allowed myself two hours to sit and read without feeling guilty. Reminding myself that I had earned this time to pause.

Being totally honest, I felt tempted to make excuses for not writing the 2000 words per week that I had committed to. It crossed my mind that Penny would not know, as I did not have to submit them to her.

The trouble with that is that we cannot lie to ourselves, and I know that my internal feeling would not have been a good one and that could have led to a full day or more of feeling bad.

> *So here I am frantically writing the 504 words before the 11 am deadline. Time 10.53 – Word count 732!*
> ***I DID IT! – Julie***

TAKE MY ADVICE

Not only do we put things off until tomorrow, but we also say things like 'I will wait until Monday / next month / after Christmas'.

Ask yourself; what am I waiting for?

Motivation is not a mythical bird that lands on your shoulder and gives you the energy you need.

Motion creates motivation, where possible tackle the head frizzle job as soon as possible.

Use the Pomodoro technique if you really cannot face starting a job. (see *Dealing with Overwhelm Chapter 8*)

Remember, thinking about doing the task makes you as tired as actually doing it!

Think how good you will feel once you have completed whichever task is causing your head frizzle

---

Bonus Advice for parents – Homework and Organisation skills

I failed miserably at this with my own children, so I am committed to getting it right with my grandchildren. I was never good at doing my homework and struggled to pay attention at school. It used to hang over me all weekend. At the last minute, I would make a half-hearted attempt to get it done or come up with a pathetic excuse for why it could not be done.

Hmmm! I feel that I have been doing the same thing with this book lately. – Julie

Do you recognise this behaviour with your own children?

Getting organised is a great habit to instil in our children while they are young. It makes for a much easier life all round and encourages better mental health. Thinking about doing something is more tortuous for your mind and body than doing it. Preparation is the key to reducing stress; for your children and you as well!

How I could have done it better

It would be wonderful if we could find a way of helping our children to enjoy their homework tasks. I would love to hear from any parents who have achieved this and will add that advice to my next book. Here are a few ideas.

- Discuss the benefits to them of getting organised and meeting deadlines.

- Set a time for your child to do their homework, preferably in a quiet space.

- Allow them some time to spend with their peers.

- If possible, have your evening meal at a set time—This is where meal prep, slow cookers and freezers come in handy. But the odd take-away, or meal out, is OK too. We are busy people.

- Help them learn to be aware of deadlines and find a way of recording them so that they get a reminder. If you have time, help them plan a homework schedule.

- Encourage them to get in the habit of preparing their school things for the next day; before they go out with friends or before bedtime. Ideally before they relax.

Chapter Three

Activate your RAS

What you need is already there for you – it's just that you can't always see it

In this chapter, we will learn how to use our thoughts and feelings effectively to help us improve our circumstances by opening us up to the possibilities that already exist for us and to help us focus on decision making and taking the right actions.

I am a great believer in the Law of Attraction, and it has often worked for me. I have heard people discount it as too 'Woo-Woo' for them. Or they say have tried it a few times, and it hasn't worked.

This is a big subject and there are many books out there full of information and practical exercises to help you explore further if it interests you. (See reading list).

There are several ways in which the Law of Attraction works; including the frequency at which you are vibrating. My focus is more on the practical engagement of your mind and how this will help you take the right actions to help you achieve what it is you are trying to create or change in your life.

Your RAS in Action

Have you ever bought a new car, or been thinking about buying a certain make or model of car and suddenly, as if by magic, loads of them appear on the roads?

Yes?

Well, that is your RAS in action.

RAS stands for Reticular Activation System. This is the part of your brain that filters out information that is unnecessary or irrelevant for you at any moment in time. It literally stops you from seeing things right in front of your eyes!

If you are interested in seeing an interesting example of how your RAS works, google 'Daniel Simons Selective Attention Test'. This is a very famous YouTube clip. I would love to know your reaction after you have watched the video!

Drop me a note at: Info@julie-monks.co.uk

As soon as something becomes a feature in your life, your RAS decides it is relevant, and you are suddenly seeing the things that you did not notice before.

I experienced this phenomenon a few years ago when my son and daughter-in-law were expecting twins.

Now, I am certain that there were twins all over the world before my twin grandson's imminent arrival. But before then, I was sure they were a rarity. Suddenly, I seemed to be surrounded by twins; there were twin strollers and prams everywhere I looked! I started a new job and several people I met mentioned that they had connections with twins.

Once my RAS was activated about the subject of twins, I started noticing what had always been there because it was now relevant to me.

A little challenge for you and your RAS

Every time you go out in a car and need to find a parking space, say to yourself, 'I always find a great parking space easily' and one will appear!

Often, I sit in the car with my husband, and he says 'I can never find a space' while we pass 3 or 4 empty spaces that he simply cannot see, because he has told his brain that they do not exist.

'Why do I need to know this?' I hear you say.

Scientists used to believe that our brains stopped improving once we reached a certain age. They also believed that our paths were pre-destined and set in stone. Nowadays, we know that this is simply not true; we can create new neurological pathways at any age, which means we can change our destiny at any point in time if that is what we truly desire.

This knowledge is invaluable for you. Whether you desire to build a successful business or career. Or if your aim is simply to improve your life.

How is this connected to the Law of Attraction, I hear you ask?

The basis is that 'what you think about you bring about'.

Whatever you focus on - good or bad — then that is what you will attract.

I have just noticed a beautiful pink rose right outside of my office window. Judging by the condition of the bloom, it has been flowering for a few days, yet I had not noticed it until now.

I have recently returned from a retreat where I learned nasal breathing. My first thought was, 'Don't we mostly breath through our noses?' But this was slightly different.

We went for a walk in the woods, and the instructor told us to keep our mouths shut and only breathe through our nose for 30 minutes.

Remember that school report I mentioned before, that said my best subject was talking? Well, this was a massive challenge for me. One that Lindsey, my mentor at the retreat, who knows me well, certainly did not expect me to comply with!

Luckily for me, I love to rise when challenged, and I found the whole experience amazing. I noticed so many things that I would not have seen if I had been chatting away like I normally would on a hike with other people. Even on a solo walk, my phone would distract me.

I could hear the birds, the crunching sound of our footsteps on the dead leaves and gravel path, even the slight breeze through the trees. Since then, I have incorporated this into a regular practice, and it is amazing how many things I notice now that I must have missed before.

The bonus is, I feel so much calmer. Because this practice activates the vagus nerve and floods our bodies with calming chemicals.

> *Penny, my extremely supportive book coach, has asked me to expand on what the vagus nerve does. When writing this, all I know was that activating it made us feel better. I was sure that they named Las Vegas after it because it was a feel-good nerve! Not true, apparently! Here is a more authoritative definition.*
> Julie

The vagus nerve is the main nerve of your parasympathetic nervous system, which controls specific body functions such as your digestion, heart rate, and immune system. These functions are involuntary, meaning you can't consciously control them.

Activate your RAS – when you need a confidence boost

Hopefully, you have had times in your life which felt amazing; where it felt that everything was going perfectly, you were loving life, and all it offered. Or other times in the past when things happened that made you feel great, accomplished, and happy.

Think about the times when you have been listening to music, and you have felt inspired and full of joy. This is down to your limbic system, which is our emotional memory. It might relate to just one minor incident where something happened perfectly, and you felt amazing afterwards.

I have a friend whose life was not going as well as she would have liked. She did not have the career she wanted and was in a lot of debt. There seemed to be no way out of her situation. She dearly wanted to get a better paid job but lacked the confidence to apply for a vacancy, let alone attend an interview. She kept telling me she had no confidence. I could clearly see that she was also telling herself that story.

'Has there ever been a time that you did something really well?' I asked.

She told me about the first time that she ever went skiing; how she had stepped on the slopes for the very first time. She skied effortlessly, all the way to the bottom, as if she had been doing it for years.

As she told me this story, her whole demeanour changed dramatically; she became enthusiastic, and her face lit up as she was describing the event. Her voice lifted; her eyes sparkled; she even stood a little straighter. You could see the change immediately. It felt magical! It was as if someone had sprinkled magic dust on her, making her feel invincible.

When she finished, I asked her how she felt, and she replied 'Amazing!' I did not need her to tell me this. It was obvious.

My advice to her was to think of this success story every time she had to do something that she was not feeling confident about. She applied this to her first job interview and got the job. This led to positive improvement in her life. Now, whenever I see her, it is lovely to see her inner sparkle.

In basic terms, our brains operate in three ways:

The *logical brain* - the part that tries to make sense of everything around us. This is apparent when we see objects in the clouds.

The *primitive or chimp brain* - the reactive part designed to keep us safe. This operates the fight, flight, or fright mode.

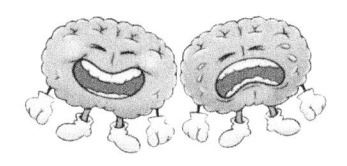

The *limbic system or emotional brain* - which we are aware of when we are recalling a past event and feel the emotion of it

Many of the problems people are facing today are due to us living in permanent stress mode, placing the *primitive brain* in control of our emotions.

Of course, if we are in a genuinely dangerous situation, for example, a crocodile is chasing us, we would want and need flight mode to be activated. Rather than the logical brain observing the situation and wondering how these creatures have evolved and questioning if it is an alligator rather than a crocodile.

At that moment we need to run for our life and let the chimp brain do its stuff.

Life is far more complicated today than it was for our primitive ancestors. Nowadays, we tend not to encounter such life threating occurrences daily. Yet we experience the same extreme levels of stress when dealing with relatively trivial situations as our ancestors did when dealing with genuinely life-threatening events.

The Limbic system is the part of the brain we can most easily influence and use as a tool to manage our stress levels effectively.

I think of it as the training brain. If we can train ourselves to use this to our advantage, then we can change how we perceive ourselves and our beliefs about our abilities.

For years, I told everyone that I was an extremely poor cook. Possibly because I did not like cooking. My story of being a terrible cook was really an excuse to let my husband do it, as he quite enjoyed cooking. As the years passed, my cooking skills became progressively worse; to the point of me burning ready meals. This was the limbic system at work, and it became a self-fulfilling prophecy.

Whatever we tell ourselves is what the brain believes.

Telling ourselves that we are bad at something creates a reality.

The good news is that this works when we tell ourselves that we are good at something, too. Many people despise the phRASe 'Fake it till you make it,' but in effect, this is what you are doing! Personally, I love that phRASe. Using it helped me to affect a massive shift in my life.

I started telling myself that I had the same opportunities as any of the most successful leaders in the company; that we all sold the same products, had the same training, and worked with the same commission plan, so there was every reason that I could succeed as well.

The company's incentive plan meant that top leaders in the company got to drive top of the range cars. So, I set myself the goal of becoming an Area Sales Manager driving a flashy Mercedes.

Every morning when I stepped out of bed, I would say to myself, 'I am Julie Monks, Area Sales Manager getting into my brand-new Mercedes.'

Then I thought, 'What would Julie be doing today to take her towards that goal?'

I also told everyone that this was my goal. (Sharing a goal or intention makes you 74% more likely to achieve it.)

What I was doing was experiencing the feeling of being successful *before* I had achieved it. By acting in that way, and experiencing those feelings of success, my whole energy and demeanour changed. As a result, I became more confident in doing the tasks that would make me a top leader in the business.

I took failure in my stride, even relished it as part of the process, and I did not let it knock my confidence or cause me to doubt my abilities. I found it easier to learn from people who had already achieved the success I was aiming for.

Within 5 months of this new mindset, my business had grown by 80%! I became an Area Sales Manager and qualified for the first level car. I felt like a different person. All because I changed the story I was telling myself.

Small confession, I continued to tell myself that I was bad at cooking for several years until I changed companies and started working for Jamie at Home, part of the Jamie Oliver group. It came back to bite me on the bum as I was selling cooking related products!

I found that being self-deprecating was not helping with my sales. Once again, it was time to tell myself a different story and become a competent cook. I would not say that I now love cooking, but I definitely cook with more confidence. I don't panic in the kitchen anymore, and we no longer eat burnt oven chips!

Activate your RAS – when you are feeling stressed or overwhelmed

Do you occasionally wake up with your gloomy goggles on?

Does everything seem negative and apathetic?

I call these days squiggle days.

When I cannot seem to get out of my own way, and my head gets crowded with pessimistic thoughts, which could be about anything. This mostly seems to happen just as the full moon is approaching.

Or maybe I can't sleep; or I wake up in the middle of the night with thoughts just swirling around my head. There are always times when you cannot seem to escape from your own thoughts.

If these are great thoughts or manifesting thoughts, then dream away. I am talking about those times when we become overwhelmed with thoughts of things we need to do or beating ourselves up about something we think we should have done differently.

Journal your RAS

I find journaling really helps.

Just getting all the stuff crowding my thoughts onto paper really helps relegate it to the filed away department in my brain. Immediately, I feel lighter and can get on with whatever it is I need to do. I rarely go back and read what I have written. This might be something to do with me not being able to read my own handwriting, but I think it is more about me getting it all out of my system.

Journaling can help you in so many ways. I even have conversations, especially arguments, with those people I know I will never confront, for whatever reason. I just get it all off my chest. Sometimes I might even burn that bit of paper. If it is something that I want to forget about; seeing it go up in flames is a wonderful way to get closure.

Activate your RAS when you need to give yourself that feel-good factor

- List the things you have been good at and have achieved in the past.

- Recall a compliment that someone gave you.

The length of your list will amaze you.

Affirmations and Afformations – Talk yourself confident

Another way in which we can activate our RAS is by using affirmations.

This is where we tell ourselves what we want to be or what we want the outcome of something to be.

I have mentioned that this is something that I have done, and it has worked for me.

For example.

Affirmation: *I am a confident person in public.*

But I know we often have a lovely little argument with ourselves when we are saying affirmations.

Straight away, the voice of the imposter person takes over and says, 'Yeah, but you're not, though, are you?' And then, unhelpfully, brings up a few reminders of times when you were lacking in confidence.

Since our brains are solution focused, we may need to consider a different approach to this.

Ask yourself, *'Why am I so confident in public?'*

When you pose your affirmation as a question, your mind looks for solutions and evidence of when you were last at ease in public.

'Remember when you spoke to a room full of people and enjoyed the experience?'

This is speaking directly to your RAS, and you will then get the feelings of being confident, which is much more likely to become a reality.

We refer to this as an AFFORMATION.

Remember! 'Why am I...?' you will shut down that pesky negative inner voice and activate your RAS positively.

Gratitude and your RAS

The biggest, most effective part of journaling is gratitude. I keep a separate book for this. Being grateful, even for the smallest things, can instantly lift your mood.

Keeping a gratitude journal is best; however, I know this can become another obstacle. Especially if you don't like to write! It becomes just another thing to add to your already overwhelming to do list.

(For more help with overwhelm, see Chapter 8 Dealing with Overwhelm)

Gratitude is a great tool to lift your mood. I learned about this process by reading The Magic by Rhonda Byrne. For the last few years, it has become a daily habit for me.

Ever since we moved to our present house, I have looked out of the window and felt grateful for the amazing view, without even realising that this small thing sets my mood for the day.

In a perfect world, we would all wake up and be grateful that we are alive. Unfortunately, this is not always the case. I can usually gauge the state of my mind by identifying what I am grateful for that morning.

On days when I am feeling deflated and have the black squiggle feeling in my chest, I find starting with the basics helps. You can say it out loud or just observe in your mind. For example,

- Thank you, that I have another day to live.
- Thank you, that I have a nice warm bed to sleep in.
- Thank you, that I have a shower and hot water to bathe in.
- Thank you, that I have a toilet, `and I do not have to poo in a hole somewhere!
- Thank you, that I have clean water on tap.
- Thank you, that I have clothes to wear.
- Thank you, that I live in a comfortable house.
- Thank you, that I can see and hear.
- Thank you for my glasses.

- Thank you, that I can read and write.
- Thank you, that I have a pen and paper.
- Thank you, that I can breathe with ease.
- Thank you, that I have soap.

There are many basic things that we can easily take for granted.

As soon as I feel gratitude in this way, it lifts my mood, and the squiggle dissipates.

Try it and see how you feel. It reminds me I live in abundance.

This is a useful exercise to use when you are in a stressful situation. Find something that you can be grateful for, even if it is something small or basic.

I discovered the magic of gratitude as a young child. There was never much money to spare, so I rarely had the things other children around me possessed. On the few occasions when I got a toy that I had coveted, I was always extremely grateful for it. I have carried this with me into adulthood.

Gratitude and the Law of Attraction

One of the easiest ways to experience the Law of Attraction and to activate your RAS is to be grateful for things that you would like to appear in your future. Whether you are looking for future success, or something more material, like a new house.

When I practiced 'fake it before I made it', this is exactly what I was doing.

Explore the feeling of the experience and the gratefulness you will feel when you turn your dreams into reality before it happens!

In my gratitude journal, I use the left side of the page for things that have already happened, and the right-hand side for advance gratitude.

For this to activate your RAS, you must act as if it has already happened and experience that feeling. Once this becomes a regular habit, opportunity will appear to be everywhere. It may even appear that things are magically appearing from nowhere.

This happens in response to your RAS being engaged, which means you are simply noticing things that have been there all along, but before you tuned in to the right frequency to see them.

Activate your RAS for a great day

How you choose to start your day makes a massive difference to how energised and productive you will be throughout the rest of the day.

Have good days and better days; the choice is yours.

Have you ever had a day when things keep going wrong?

'I must have got out of the wrong side of the bed this morning.'

'If it can go wrong, it will go wrong.'

The day starts badly, and then you have run out of coffee.

You spill something on your clothes; you have mislaid your keys (notice that I say mislaid rather than lost.); the dog won't come in when he's called; and then when you get in the car, maybe you find you are low on fuel.

The temptation is to say. 'I am having a bad day.'

But once you utter this phRASe, I can guarantee that your day will get worse.

Why? Because you have activated your RAS!

Once you have told yourself that you are going to have a bad day, then your RAS will look for evidence to ensure that you do.

I have learned to stop a bad day in its tracks by telling myself that although a few annoying things have occurred, the day will improve.

Once I was running late and typically needed fuel. By the time I arrived at the petrol station, I was a bit agitated and rushed to put the nozzle into the car. Nothing. The attendant was nowhere to be seen, and she hadn't switched the pump on.

Eventually, she strolled back into the garage and leisurely switched on the pump. By this point, I felt really frustrated and angry too. Before I walked in to pay, I paused, took a deep breath, and said, 'I am having a good day. Make sure she has one, too.'

I plastered a smile on my face, was extremely polite, and thanked her.

She told me she was having a disastrous day, and that was why she had kept me waiting. With that, I told her it would get better from now on and left feeling much lighter and positive about my day. Hopefully, it had the same effect on her.

Imagine if I had gone in there and ranted. One; I would have made her day a lot worse, which is not a nice thing to do. Two; I would have felt bad and guilty as soon I as I got back into the car.

TAKE MY ADVICE

Tell yourself that today is going to be a good day.

When you lose something, tell yourself that you have mislaid it rather than lost it. Think back to when you were last in possession of said item.

Activate your RAS when you awake

I was never a morning person and used to joke that any time getting out of bed was too early for me. I never woke up feeling refreshed, and although I functioned and got through the day, I often struggled. This left me feeling that I achieved nothing, and I would be frantically working long into the night to catch up.

We all have different energy patterns; some of us are night owls while others are larks. Unfortunately, unless you work for yourself and can choose your own schedule, most of the stuff we need to do in the Western world revolves around daylight hours. There is also well-documented research on the benefits of natural daylight.

There are many books about the benefits of morning rituals. One of my favourites is Miracle Morning by Hal Elrod. Most prescribed morning routines include meditation, reading, exercise and journaling. The Miracle Morning is my favourite because it is very flexible. You can set your own time scale and even pare it down to just a few minutes if needed.

Of course, this might be more difficult if you have young children! But there is always a way to incorporate this into your life. The premise is that a morning routine sends a message to you that says; I am in control and ready to start the day!

If you create your own little routine, there will be less temptation to return to bed to grab that extra little snooze, especially if you make your bed as soon as you get out of it. It is also the first accomplishment of the day.

My ideal morning routine comprises:

- Meditation.
- Affirmations or Afformations - whichever suits you best.
- Movement - choose what feels comfortable and invigorating for you.
- Reading - choose something uplifting and inspirational.

There is nothing better than feeling accomplished and energised before you start your day.

I like to think of my morning routine as plugging myself into the good mood charger.

It's important that the routine includes stuff that lifts your energy and your vibration. This varies from person to person.

Morning routine simple swaps

Swap your first coffee for warm water and lemon, as this helps cleanse the liver and will help you feel less sluggish.

Drink half a pint of water as soon as you wake, I keep a glass by my bedside.

Swap your morning scroll through your social media for a chapter of an education or inspirational book.

This would also be an ideal time to do some gratitude, either by journaling it or simply saying it to yourself. Whichever works best for you.

Avoid reading or watching the news first thing in the morning. It rarely lifts your mood.

Swap your 15 mins snooze time for some form of movement – it could be anything from vigorous housework to dancing to your favourite tunes. The idea is to get sweaty as this activates those neurons in the brain.

If you are not used to exercise, start with 5 minutes, and build up. This will benefit both mind and body as it gets the blood pumping round your system.

Take my advice

An hour is usually the ideal time for a brilliant morning routine. If you struggle to get out of bed, then start by waking up 15 minutes earlier than you usually would. Gradually increase this in increments of 15 minutes until you can achieve an hour.

Aim to get up without snoozing if you can. For some of us, it seems hard. But the longer you lounge under the duvet, the harder it becomes.

Clean your teeth and throw some cold water on your face. I bet you are feeling more energised by simply thinking about doing this.

You don't need to follow any fixed order for whatever you choose to do afterwards. You will soon figure out works best and is most effective for you. It might seem strange, but I walk around my bedroom clapping; I have since read that this lifts the energy in a room (Feng Shui).

Finally, and importantly. A word of warning.

Introduce a new morning routine gently. DO NOT use it as a stick to beat yourself with.

Even getting up 15 minutes earlier than usual is an achievement!

There are many tweaks you can make to personalise your morning routine.

It is about starting your day with energy and good intentions.

For those of you who have absolutely no intention of attempting a morning routine, may I suggest you try this one thing whatever time you wake.

Start every day with gratitude, even if you can only find one thing to be grateful for. It will have an amazing and positive impact on your life.

Oh, and you might like to try the clapping too. – Julie

Put it out there!

One of my favourite phRASes is 'Put it out there. Or don't put it out there.'

Whoops! Take the don't out of that sentence!

What you focus on is what you attract, good or bad. I see it as the message you are projecting into the universe, as your words subconsciously activate your RAS.

Positive words influence positive actions.

When speaking, talk about the things you want to happen in your life, or a particular outcome as opposed to what you don't want to happen.

With any undertaking, it is important that you imagine a great outcome, as you are more likely to influence the right actions.

Activate your RAS...

- On awakening

- When you need to improve your situation

- When you want to manifest

- Before you go for a job interview

- When you have mislaid something

- When you are looking for a parking space

- When you are setting any kind of goal

- When you are shopping and need to find something specific

- When you are feeling tired and need an energy boost

- When you have a head Fizzle task

- Remind yourself of what you are capable of, rather than focusing on what you fear

- When you want to feel better

This is my take on the Law of Attraction.

There are three elements needed for the Law of Attraction to work

Focus

Energy

Action

In this chapter, I have focused on using your RAS to see the possibilities and the opportunities that already exist, although you may not be aware of them yet.

Using your RAS will help direct your energies towards the action needed to manifest your desires.

Have fun activating your RAS to your advantage.

Chapter Four

Did you say what I think you said?

The importance of good communication

'Is that what you said? – That's not what I heard you say!'

Lack of communication or miscommunication creates so many problems. We need to know what to expect and what is expected of us.

We often underestimate the power of both the spoken, and the written word.

Most relationship problems and even, if I may be so bold, many world problems result from poor communication.

All work and personal relationships are reliant on good communication.

A big part of this problem is a lack of listening skills. I am sure this causes many disagreements. Let me hold my hand up and say that I am guilty of this, too.

Let's look at some ways this becomes an issue.

- Interrupting the flow of a conversation by second guessing what the other person is going to say and jumping in before they have completed their sentence. How often have you heard someone say, "We get on so well that we finish each other's sentences."

That may seem cute, but boy, can it be annoying! Inevitably, the listener makes the wrong guess, which is infuriating, as the speaker then needs to repeat the sentence. The speaker also feels frustrated as all they to do is finish their sentence without interruption.

- Not engaging fully when another person is speaking to you. For example, being distracted by your phone or not looking in their direction when they are talking to you.

- Not listening, because you are waiting for your opportunity to speak.

- Jumping in with what happened to you when they are trying to tell you a story.

- Not delivering the message to the correct person.

- Not asking questions when you don't fully understand what is being said to you.

Are you talking to the right person?

One interesting phenomenon which often ends with disastrous results is when someone does not give the message to the correct recipient; the person who needs to know.

This might happen because we are wary of the reaction we might receive when we deliver the message. Particularly when the message contains bad news. We feel the urge to discuss the outcome with someone else, to gain feedback about the situation within the message, before delivering it to the correct person.

Something else to consider here; although you may think you have explained something well, the recipient may have heard the message differently.

Take My advice

Deliver the message directly to the intended recipient first. There is nothing worse than finding out something second hand, especially when it is specific or important to you.

If you are sharing important instructions, make sure you deliver them straight to the person or persons involved, as the message can get lost in translation. Best practice is to give important instructions in writing.

It is also wise to ask them to confirm what you have said, as it helps you ensure they understand exactly what is expected of them.

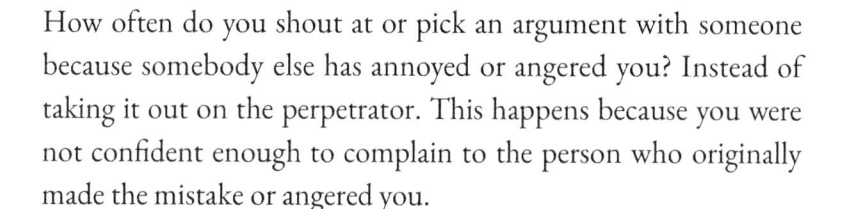

How often do you shout at or pick an argument with someone because somebody else has annoyed or angered you? Instead of taking it out on the perpetrator. This happens because you were not confident enough to complain to the person who originally made the mistake or angered you.

Here's an example of this behaviour from my husband, Dave.

What a gift he is to this book!

He picks up our takeout meal and discovers they have given him the wrong order. He gets home and shouts at me. No matter how well I keep myself under control, him shouting at me has activated my chimp brain, especially as I am hangry*. So now I am shouting back at him! Or if I somehow resist that urge, I am still in a state of heightened alert.

* Hungry and angry.

Where possible, save your venting for the person concerned. If you really feel that you need to offload your day's frustrations onto somebody else, then try to relay the story in a calm tone of voice, even if you are still caught up in the emotion you felt when the event took place. Trust me on this - it will make for an easier life in the long run.

Many a true word spoken in jest

'I'm not being funny but....'

'I'm not being rude but...'

If you start a conversation with phrases like these, it is highly unlikely that you will follow it up by saying something nice!

Now that I have pointed this out, you will notice when you use phrases like this or if other people use them in conversation with you.

There is a good reason for this that you can learn more about in Chapter 3. Activating your RAS

Take My Advice

Be aware if you are speaking in this way. We need to be careful of our words. Understanding this can help you recognise what people are really saying to you!

Take the 'Don't' out of that sentence

Watch a young child, happily walking along with a drink in their hand, without spilling a drop. Then, an adult, mindful of their pristine flooring, says those fateful words; 'Don't spill it!'

Fearful now, the child becomes nervous, his hands shake, and he spills the drink.

Until someone mentioned it, the child hadn't even thought about spilling the drink! The adult planted that picture in their mind.

Here are a few classics.

'Don't drink too much tonight'.

– Great idea! Wasn't planning to, but now you've put the idea in my head…

'Don't trip over that step'.

- What step? Oops!

'Don't think of a pink elephant'.

'Don't touch that'.

– Ouch! You've burned yourself!

I am reminded of a British TV soap series called Keeping Up Appearances. The main character, Hyacinth Bucket (pronounced Bouquet!) put the fear of God in her timid neighbour, Elizabeth, every time she handed her one of her best china cups.

'Don't break it dear' she would say, 'that's my best Royal Doulton you know!'

Immediately Elizabeth would start shaking, setting the cup rattling precariously in the saucer.

Something that always makes me chuckle crops up mainly when people post memes on social media.

'I don't give a F*** about what others think of me.'

Take the 'don't' out of that sentence and see what it says.

It is interesting to tune in and listen to what people are really saying. This is even more important when applied to self-talk. The things you say to yourself can have a profound effect.

'Discussion is an exchange of knowledge; argument an exchange of ignorance.' - Robert Quillen

Choose your battles wisely

We all have those people in our lives who will disagree with anyone and everything. We frequently exhaust ourselves, being angry inside and out, because we know we are right, and we want everyone to see it our way.

Well, some people are just plain stubborn, and we must learn to accept that.

Ask yourself; is it so important to be right? What difference does it make?

Unless someone's opinion is going to endanger their life or, more importantly, yours, then just let them get on with it. They will learn the hard way.

A great phrase comes to mind.

'A man convinced against his will is of the same opinion still.'

- *Dale Carnegie- How to win friends and influence people.*

If, after reading this, you still feel the need to make another person see something in a different light, then the best way to do so is to start by asking questions.

For example, let look at something that happened a lot when I worked in direct sales.

'That's pyramid selling, that is.' people would sneer.

In my early days I would get very defensive and waste a good 10 mins of their time, and mine, explaining that was not the case. Only to watch them go off, still believing they were right and feeling that they had made their point rather than me making mine.

It took me a long time to figure out that I was exactly like them! Always thinking that I was right. Immoveable in my opinions.

Once I began learning from immensely successful people, I changed my approach. I started asking questions:

'Can you explain your understanding of what Pyramid selling is to me, and do you think it is a good thing or a bad thing?'

If they said it was bad, I would ask them to explain to me exactly what they believed was bad about it.

'Have you ever had any experience of Pyramid selling? Tell me about it.'

I found this gave me more of an opportunity to explain my point of view. Then I could give them examples of the difference between direct sales and pyramid selling.

Because I had asked for their thoughts and listened to what they said, they were more likely to listen to me, which helped them form a different opinion.

Acting in this way gives them the opportunity to feel that you have helped them make an informed decision, rather than them feeling that you have forced your views on them.

You do not have to show up to every argument you receive an invitation to. A friend of mine, Linda Emmott, has a phrase for this, 'It's not a hill to die on.'

Basically – you need to pick your battles. These days I always ask myself 'Is this one worth the stress? 'What will it cost you?'

You can apply these questions to most things.

How often do we waste time and energy arguing or fighting just to prove a point? We need to be honest with ourselves about why we are pursuing any battle and what will be the benefit to us if we win.

Allen Pease, the Australian body language expert and author, says,

> 'People have two motivations when they do things. Make a gain or avoid a pain.'

So tell me:

- What is your reason?

- Is it going to be worth the emotional toil in the end?

- On a scale of 1-10, how important is the outcome to you personally?

All that said, there is always the odd occasion when I feel I must make a comment or have the last word when someone is rude to me.

For the people that know me, I feel I should add a LOL here! – Julie

If I am dealing with a rude person, I love to say, 'You are very rude!' in a calm voice with a massive smile. The look I receive in return is priceless.

Which brings me nicely to my next subject.

Listening - Remember to fully engage

I used to ask a room full of delegates, 'Who is the most important person to you?'

The answers would range from my children; my partner; my siblings; or my parents.

I have news for you! It is *none* of them.

The person who is most important to you is YOU! Yes - YOU!

When you see a group photograph, who is the first person you look for?

Believe me, I am 100% right about this.

Why don't we see this?

For those of us that grew up pre-1990s, the answer probably lies in our upbringing. Especially if you were part of the Brownie/Scout movement, which instructed us to think of others before we thought of ourselves.

'Get to the point, Julie!' I hear you say. What does this have to do with listening and why is it so beneficial to us to listen to what others have to say?

Remember, the person you know the most about is YOU. If there were a university degree in self-knowledge, you would have achieved a first.

People feel confident talking about themselves because they have all the knowledge; they know all the answers. In fact, they wrote the course! In that position, we feel safe because we know our subject inside and out.

By listening properly to another person, you help them feel secure and confident. They are more likely to build a rapport with you and listen to you too. Often, we do not listen properly to what other people are saying because we are too busy looking for a gap in the conversation so that we can say our piece.

I have a friend who is a genuinely nice person and would do anything for anyone. Yet lots of people really dislike her. I used to wonder why until I started spending more time with her. She rarely allows you to get halfway through a sentence, let alone to the end of it!

We want to be heard. It is human nature. The best compliment you can give to someone is to listen to them properly and respond to what they are saying.

When a person is sharing their personal experience, it feels natural to jump in and respond with 'Yes, that happened to me.'

But they are not bloody interested in what happened to you. They just want to share their story. Nothing is more frustrating than being interrupted when you are in full flow.

Over the years, I have witnessed many unpleasant situations that could have been avoided if only the other person had paid attention and acted appropriately.

Ask yourself; how many mistakes have you made because of only half listening? Or deciding for yourself what you think the other person is saying?

Let people have their moment – Conversation is not a contest

Often, in our quest to make people like us or to get into rapport with another person, we find ourselves in a competitive conversation.

We do this by attempting to align ourselves and find common ground. This can become annoying to the other person when they are telling you something about themselves.

There they are, in full flow of their story, brimming with emotion (this could range from enthusiasm to anger) and BANG! You jump straight in and interrupt them. They may be talking about anything; from their children, a minor achievement or something massive in their lives.

We feel that our mission to find common ground and insert our story or a similar achievement takes precedence over them finishing their sentence. This might be done with the best of intentions. The worst-case scenario is when we consciously or unconsciously go for one-upmanship.

It is so tempting, when a person shares an experience with you, to rush in and tell them exactly how you have experienced something similar. This can deprive them of their moment of glory or drama.

When we jump in, it is often to tell them how our situation was far worse or far more dramatic than theirs. Mistakenly, we think this will make them feel better. Sadly, what it does is leave them feeling deflated. It could even make them dislike you at that moment.

All they want to do is to tell you their story and for you to listen and comment accordingly.

When someone is experiencing a difficult time or situation, the last thing they want to hear is what happened to you in the past, even if relevant to their situation. They mostly just want someone to listen and empathise so that they can unburden themselves. Remember, the most important person in everyone's life is themselves.

If they have come to you for advice, however, that is a different matter. Although I would offer a word of caution here. I suggest that before you offer any advice on any subject; you get permission before you give it. It is important to remember that mostly when people are asking for advice, what they are really expecting is for you to agree with a decision that they have already made. The secret is to always listen first.

As it says in Stephen R Covey's book, 'The 7 habits of Highly Effective People' –

'Seek first to understand, before being understood'.

We need to let people have their moment and give them the space to have their say.

Take My Advice

Really listen, without thinking about what you are going to say when they take a breath.

Empathise, but do not take over the conversation.

If they are speaking about an achievement, then give them genuine praise.

If you are going to offer advice, ask their permission first.

Let people decide for themselves

This is an urban myth, yet I believe it happened to my husband for real.

After many years of spending hundreds of pounds on repairs every summer, our lawn mower finally gave up the ghost. Our grass was getting longer and longer. Our newish neighbour had recently purchased a brand-new shiny ride-on mower, and we could hear the motor running as he meandered around his garden.

'Shall I go round and ask him if I can borrow his mower?' Dave asked me.

Before I could answer, he followed up with several more comments.

It went something like:

'I doubt if he will lend it to me, it's brand new'.

'He will not lend it to me'.

'I can't ask him'.

In the urban myth, the man has several conversations in his head ending with him knocking on his neighbour's door and telling him to shove his lawnmower where the sun doesn't shine!

Even though this was the very first time he had spoken to the neighbour!

Of course, his neighbour was completely baffled by this interaction as no one had ever approached him to borrow his mower in the first place!

Back to our story. After we spent a small fortune on a brand new, shiny, red, all-singing, all-dancing lawn mower, our neighbour commented on how lovely our new machine was.

Dave told him that before purchasing one, he had considered asking to borrow his. 'Oh, I wish you had,' our neighbour exclaimed, 'I would even have cut your grass for you, as I was loving playing with my new toy.'

A lesson learned!

As much as it would be very useful for us to know what other people are thinking, we can never know how someone will react to a question or request.

It took me a long time to understand that not everyone thinks the same as me. Yet what kind of world would it be if we thought the same?

I have lost count of the opportunities lost because I did not ask or because I decided I knew what the other person was thinking.

This was one of the major hurdles I needed to overcome to find success in the direct sales industry.

Before social media, the best way to recruit and grow a team was to invite potential recruits to find out more about your business.

This was something I struggled with for the first 2 years of working in the industry. I became a consultant with the Virgin Cosmetics brand as soon as adverts for the role started appearing in newspapers and magazines.

Wrongly, I assumed everyone was just like me. I thought that if I included my recruitment spiel after my make-over demo, they would all ask me if they could become a consultant and join my team.

After two years with the company, I had built a small team of like-minded consultants who had asked me about the business opportunity. But while I had a team of six, there were other leaders who had built huge teams with hundreds of consultants in their down line in the same time span.

'What was I doing so wrong?' I asked myself.

I was extremely enthusiastic, hard-working, and dedicated many hours to growing my business. After attending yet another seminar, I took the bold step of asking the most successful leaders what they did to grow such big businesses in such a short space of time.

The answer was universal.

'I ask *everyone;* and let them make their own decision about the business.'

I realised my problem was that I was taking the decision out of my potential consultant's hands by making assumptions.

For example, I met an extremely busy lady called Deb. She had two children, worked full time and was studying for an honour's degree. To top it all, she was not that interested in make-up either. I nearly discounted her by assuming that she would be far too busy to become a consultant with everything she had going on in her life.

I even asked her sister, as she seemed a much more likely candidate. Luckily for me, Deb contacted me a few months later and signed up to become a consultant. She reached the top level of Executive Sales Manager and built one of the most successful businesses within the company.

I had learned my lesson. From then on, I offered the opportunity to everyone I spoke to. Only a small percentage of those I asked agreed to join; but it was enough to build a business with a five-million-pound turnover (this was in 2006).

I can hear you saying, 'Yeah, but what about the people who said no?'

It is true, there were many people who said no. But – most of them felt pleased to be asked, flattered by the thought that I believed they could do what I was doing.

I have many other examples of this form of miscommunication – assuming I know how other people feel.

Even the recent experience of planning my husband's 60th birthday party. As we put together the guest list, he kept saying things like,

'It's probably too far for them to come.'

I was literally screaming at him to just ask them and let them make up their own minds.

Let's look at this from another perspective. How would you like other people making your decisions for you?

Take My Advice

If you want to ask someone something; whether it is a favour, or you simply want them to go somewhere with you. Whatever the reason. Just ask!

Then let them be in control of their decision. You may be amazed by their response, saving yourself many hours of agonising!

What is the worst that can happen? They might say no; but if they do, at least you will know the outcome and can proceed from there.

To detail or not to detail

Being a good listener is a must if you are in sales or even if you want to make new friends. It is useful to observe the amount of detail people include when they tell a personal story or are recalling an event.

Some people love to hear every little twist, turn and deviation of a saga whereas others, me included, just need to hear the bare bones.

Often, when my husband is telling me about something to do with the business, he walks and talks all around the issue, when all I want is to hear the outcome and the actions we need to take. Because of this, I call him Detail Dave.

This skill can be invaluable. For instance, when any kind of inspector arrives at our workplace, I know Dave will supply all the information required. However, his attention to detail can also infuriate people.

People love talking, and they cannot wait to get their point of view across. Having great listening skills pays dividends.

- How is the other person's narrative?
- Are they giving you lots of detail?
- Or do they get straight to the point?

Of course, we also need to take the circumstances of the conversation into account. Is it a friendly chit chat or a business conversation? The secret is to match their style.

Or be straight up. Ask them if they would like to hear the finer details. I sometimes ask them directly if they are a detail person or not.

At other times, the situation will dictate the number of details needed. Particularly if it is a life-or-death instruction.

> *Just after I finished writing this chapter, Dave gifted me another great example! – Julie*

I was approaching the shops and called Dave to ask if he had got anything for his lunch.

Me: 'Dave, have you bought anything for lunch yet?'

Dave: 'I've not long been home from work, I have just taken the dogs out and I have to go to Phil's farm and look at a job then I had to get the trailer ready for Roy to pick up, the traffic was really bad...'

For goodness' sake! All I needed was a 'Yes' or a 'No'!

Another classic.

Dave: 'I'm driving. I can't really talk; the traffic is really bad, I'm just going under the railway bridge at Westerleigh, you know by the garden centre...'

Just ignore the bloody call!

I really do not need the detail.

Tone of voice and the written word

The perfect way to hold a conversation is face to face. In person. We benefit from hearing the tone of voice and can read the other person's body language, along with their facial expressions.

It is said that millennials prefer to speak via the medium of the written word rather than use their voice. But the problem with the written word is that there is no tone of voice. We assume that the recipient of the message is reading it in the same tone we used when we wrote it, but this may not be true!

The recipient chooses the tone of voice when they are reading the message. How they perceive the message will be influenced by their mood and their circumstances when they receive it. So be mindful of this when you are sending written communication.

Try some of these questions in different tones of voice and see how differently they come across.

- What have you been doing today?
- Have you done that job that I asked you to do?
- Are you going to watch the football all day?
- Have you cut the grass?

Interesting how different those questions sound in different tones of voice.

You cannot predict how another person will react, but it is worth bearing in mind that the recipient may interpret your message differently from its written form. Conversely, you may also misinterpret the tone of voice in the messages that you receive.

Take my advice

Keep in mind that the writer may use a different tone of voice when writing a message compared to the one you hear in your head. Try it out in a different tone if it has annoyed you.

When you receive a message that has angered you, wait 24 hours before replying.

Truly engage in the listening process and let others finish their sentences before you speak. Try to respond to what they have been saying. One great way to do this is to repeat back some of what they have just told you.

Use receptive body language when listening, such as nodding and mirroring their stance.

Let people have their moment of glory or drama, avoiding engaging in a competitive conversation.

Not everyone is interested in the finer details of a story.

If asking a question, do not assume what the answer will be until you receive it.

Really listen – I cannot stress this enough.

Chapter Five

The Business of Work

Life skills for business; business skills for life!

> *Find a job you love, and you will never have to work a day in your life'.*

This often-used quote has been attributed to lots of different people, including Confucius, Mark Twain, and Steve Jobs!

When you consider how much time most of us spend at work, it seems like a good idea, for our own sanity, to make it a pleasant experience.

> *Although this chapter focuses on work and business, there are some great life skill tips worth reading in here! – Julie*

For most of my working life, I have been self-employed or running my own business in one form or another. I have experienced success and failure and learned the value of hindsight!

As with most of the topics in this book, I am sharing the lessons I have learned. My book is not a comprehensive guide to work and business. There are plenty of books already written on this subject, some of which I have found immensely helpful. I have included my favourites in my reading list at the back of the book.

Most of the businesses I have been involved in are what I call 'people' businesses, where I have had direct contact with the customer. Yet, I have also found this experience valuable when dealing with staff and colleagues in other work situations.

Since the pandemic, remote working has become more popular. If you are used to the structure of a workplace, it can be difficult shifting to working from home. Self-discipline is key, especially if you are self-employed.

Working from home

This presents many distractions. Here are a few of my personal tips to help you stay on track and not feel overwhelmed with all the tasks on your to-do list.

- Whenever possible, start work at the same time every day. I used to work with a lady who would leave her house and walk round the block to put herself into work mode before she entered her home office.

- Have a dedicated, organised workspace. Give it a fun name - I always say, "I am entering the money-making room. "Dave says he is going to the "lucrative workshop."

- Turn all social media notifications to silent. I guarantee that there won't be anything important you'll miss.

- Discipline yourself to only check your emails three times a day, unless you are expecting something important or relevant to your current task. Book this into your schedule every day. Only reply to the ones that need immediate attention.

- Focus solely on the task that you are working on. Book in working times and do not be distracted by household tasks.

- Set your working hours. They can be flexible each day, depending on your commitments. I achieve more by starting my working day at 10 am. This means I can put in a load of washing and do a quick tidy up before starting work. Once I start, I focus fully on that until 2.30 pm, when it is time for the school run. I treat it in the same way as if I am working for an employer. As soon as I enter my study, I am at work.

Interruptions

One of the biggest downsides of working from home is that your friends and family know you are at home and believe it is okay to drop in for a quick coffee and chat.

This freedom can be a huge positive if you are working for yourself. One of the main reasons people choose self-employment is that they love the freedom and flexibility that it brings. I know I do.

But if you are working to a deadline or have lots to get through, these distractions can become a real problem.

Take my advice

We never want to be rude or offend anyone, but sometimes needs must and we have to be firm.

My advice?

When you answer the door, instead of stepping back and inviting them in, step out of the door towards them and explain kindly that it is lovely to see them, but you are in your working hours and on a tight deadline. Unfortunately, you cannot take a break at that moment. Then arrange a different time to suit you both.

Taking on other people's tasks and how to say no

Are you a people pleaser? I know I am. This trait often leads to us prioritising other people's tasks and favours ahead of our own. In the short term, this provides us with an instant hit of altruism, the feel-good factor of being generous with our time and helping someone out.

But the downside is that we risk feeling overwhelmed and resentful. If it is your boss or your employer asking you to do something extra, you will feel obliged. But it does not always have to be that way.

I remember a big conference where I had to handle several presentations and take charge of a significant part of the event organisation. I had a lot on my plate and then my boss asked me to write another presentation. Being an excellent employee, I did not question it and spent half the night writing and rehearsing it.

Next day, when we arrived ready for the conference, he told me it was no longer needed. I was fuming, although slightly relieved that there was less to do.

Could this have been managed in a more effective way?

TAKE MY ADVICE

Someone gave me a brilliant piece of advice on this topic; it works every time. If it is no problem; you have time and you are more than happy to do the extra task, then go ahead.

There is nothing to be gained from adopting a jobsworth attitude.

If you feel that doing something extra and/or working to a deadline could compromise the extra task, then speak up. Respond by saying:

'I would love to do this X task but that will mean that I cannot do this Y task. Which one would you like me to prioritise?'

Your tone of voice is important in this situation. Keep it neutral. This diplomatic response is polite and constructive, leaving both parties satisfied with the outcome.

'Deciding what not to do is as important as deciding what to do.' –Jessica Jackley, businesswoman.

Some people see delegation as failure. They like to be in total control of everything. I expect you have heard the saying, 'If you want a job doing properly, then do it yourself.'

This is not always the best solution!

If you dislike doing something – pay someone else to do it.

Believe it or not, you are not always the best person for the job. Sometimes you need to hire an expert. There are only 24 hours in a day. Spread yourself too thin, and you end up feeling frazzled and out of control.

> *I can hear you saying, 'What is she talking about? I can't afford that!'. Read on so I can explain.* – Julie

Rarely does anything good happen when you put things off - unless it is the washing up and my husband gets so sick of the sight of it, he does it himself!

There was a time when I was 5 years behind with my bookkeeping. There was a massive box stuffed full of receipts and other bits I thought I might need, but I kept thinking, 'I haven't got the time now; I'll sort them out soon.'

But I never found find the time! Then, £100 fines started arriving monthly. I was exhausted, just thinking about doing the work, and it became one of my daily head fizzles.

When I eventually got around to attempting to sort it out, I tried starting at the beginning, but I got into more of a mess and the task seemed impossible. I really could not remember what had taken place 5 years ago. (This was pre-personal accounting software).

I was busy, and my business was taking off. Then it occurred to me I was making more money per hour than my accountant would charge me to get the books brought up to date. I handed him the box and let him work his magic. It was worth every penny to have a clearer head, allowing me to focus on the much more important task of growing my business.

Sometimes you must delegate; we cannot be good at everything - especially when there is a job we dislike doing. Weigh up the pros and cons. In this example, it was going to incur a cost, yet ultimately it left me time to create more income without the worry of the inland revenue chasing me and charging me penalties!

Housework is another thing that is easy to delegate. Working in a cluttered and disorganised environment is not conducive to doing great work. It is also a source of endless distraction, as you are constantly aware of the things that need doing, especially when working from home. Think what you could do with that extra time and extra head space if you hired a cleaner.

I would rather be an idiot driving a nice car! Sometimes we just need to do the job that scares us

Success is personal and involves being prepared to do whatever it takes to achieve it.

For me, the absolute pinnacle of success in the company I was working with was the offer of a smart new car, part of the company incentive program. When you reached a certain level of team sales and maintained them for a defined period, this car was your reward.

When this incentive was first introduced, I found it inspirational. It switched my focus. I realised that to achieve this reward, I would need to do all the tasks I had been avoiding because they scared me. The main one being cold calling.

Why was I afraid of it?

Mainly because of my fear of ridicule. I was terrified that other people would think I was an idiot. To earn the reward I craved, I was going to have to take that risk.

I coined the phrase 'I would rather be an idiot driving a nice car' and told myself this every time I had to do a scary task. Every time I said it, it instantly focused me on the reward rather than my fear and made the task enjoyable.

My experience taught me that to make progress, we must do the things that scare us or that we dislike doing.

Back in the day, before social media, we had to make cold sales calls and few people like doing those. Even worse, our superiors expected us to engage in cold canvassing, which I really despised. I made every excuse to myself and my boss to explain why I could not do it. Again, the main thing stopping me was fear.

Fear of ridicule; fear of failure; fear that someone would slam the door in my face.

Luckily for me, I happened upon a book called 'Questions are the Answers' by an Australian body language expert and author, Allan Pease. This book included a formula for knocking on doors.

The two main things that I learned were.

#1 It is a numbers game; for every 10 people you speak to, 3 will listen to what you are offering, and 1 will accept it.

#2 If ever someone said the dreaded NO word to me, it would not kill me and that I would forget about it as soon as I focused on asking the next person. For me, the word NO became Next Opportunity.

I learnt to focus on the task rather than the result. Hey! Not only was I going to focus on the task, but I was also bloody well going to enjoy executing it!

I told myself and a colleague that today our job was to collect as many Nos as possible. That was our only focus and when we had reached 10 in a row, without a single yes in between, then we could have a cake and a cup of tea.

Surprisingly, not one person was rude or slammed the door in our faces and we never once achieved 10 No's in a row. From that day on, we planted seeds, and I eventually built one of the biggest teams in the region.

The lesson I learned from this was:

'If you want something enough, you must be prepared to do whatever it takes to get your desired results.'

If it is legal, of course!

Under promise and over deliver – do what you say you are going to do

Whether it's your job or your business, maintaining an excellent reputation is essential for gaining and keeping customers. There is nothing worse than letting your clients down.

I believe this happens because we hate upsetting people. So, we avoid telling them something we think might disappoint them.

Like the builder who tells the customer that they will be round in 2 weeks' time because he thinks they might go elsewhere if he cannot fit them in sooner. Knowing full well that realistically it will be more like 4 weeks before he can get to them. Or when a company promises that your order will arrive by a certain date, then cannot deliver it on time.

In the long run, all this does is cause more upset. But more importantly, it damages your reputation. If you are in business and you are great at what you do, then you are going to be busy. This means it may take a while to fit a new customer in.

Personally, I would rather trust a busy tradesperson who cannot accommodate me for a while over one who can slot me in straight away. Be honest with your customers. Give them a realistic time slot and, wherever possible, stick to it.

I know that this is not always possible, especially in the building trade where you may be at the mercy of the weather, or hairdressing where your previous client's appointment might take longer than you expected.

It is far better to tell the truth and keep the customer informed before any changes.

If you are going to keep them waiting for 30 minutes, then tell them 35 or even 40! That way, if you get to them sooner, you will have a happy customer. There is nothing worse than being told you have a 10-minute wait, which then turns out to be more like 30 minutes.

This is also important in personal situations. Many arguments in relationships could be avoided if people do what they say they are going to do at the time they said they were going to do it.

In both business and personal situations, no one is interested in your excuses. Far better not to make promises at all than to make them and renege on them.

The power of the pause

Occasionally, during business, we receive a snotty or angry message. It may come via any messaging medium. In my case, it is usually an email. The temptation is to reply immediately, but if you do this, it is likely that your reply will also be angry. This will not resolve the situation and often may even exacerbate it.

Remember that written messages have the disadvantage of potentially losing their true meaning in 'textation'. We cannot hear the tone of voice or see the expression on a person's face, which makes it easy to misconstrue the message.

TAKE MY ADVICE

If possible, wait at least 24 hours before replying as by then you will have calmed down and will deliver a more rational reply. This is far more likely to help with resolving the situation.

Better late than never

'Better three hours too soon than a minute too late.' –
William Shakespeare

When is it ok to be late?

Never in my book. Of course, there are always occasions when lateness is unavoidable. A road accident or an unexpected last-minute crisis. But for many of us, being late has become a habit. I have observed that most people who show up late to gatherings rarely do so quietly. They tend to crash in noisily, creating disruption for those who were punctual.

In my humble opinion, being late shows a total lack of respect for other people. Incredibly, I know some people who are proud of the fact that they are always late, even making a joke about it.

No-one is interested in your excuses. By the time you arrive, they will feel frustrated or even angry. How do I know this? Well, I was one of those people who was consistently 30 minutes late for everything. Unless I had to catch a plane or a train. Somehow, then, I could always be punctual.

I read about this in a book called Being Happy by Andrew Matthews.

This was me; always late to meetings, arriving in a whirlwind with a multitude of lame excuses. The plain unattractive truth was that I had made a choice - to be late.

My boss was not interested in my excuses. She was annoyed that her meeting had been disrupted and that it would now run over. All thanks to me and my disregard for the other attendees, who had all shown up on time.

One of my daughters-in-law was always a minimum of an hour late for everything! I got in the habit of telling her that a family meal was scheduled for an hour earlier than it was. Her excuse was that she had six children to get ready. Even though one of them had left home, and another was a teenager, quite able to look after herself and help with the younger ones.

Eventually, I raised this with her, saying 'Well, you knew you had six children yesterday, didn't you?'

All she had to do was to allow more time!

Yes, I am probably the nightmare mother-in-law I never intended to be! But it was always chaos when she arrived and on this Mother's Day, our table was only available for a short time. Her lateness not only affected our assembled family, who were waiting for over an hour, but also kept the family who had booked the table after us waiting.

Take my advice

Aim to always arrive at least 10 minutes early for a meeting. If it is an important meeting, then aim for 30 minutes.

If you are driving or travelling by public transport, allow extra travel time. Yes, you may end up wasting time waiting around, but this is better than offending people.

Prepare the evening before. Choose and lay out your clothes; ensure that you have everything you need, packed and ready to go.

PEOPLE SKILLS - Make people feel important

The customer does not care about how your day is going.

If you are in a position where you deal with customers directly; whether face to face, over the phone or any kind of written interaction, remember that regardless of how good or bad your day is going, the customer expects, and is entitled to, a good experience.

They do not care about what is happening in your life; they are only interested in their own. It is important that they have a brilliant experience, no matter how you are feeling and vitally important that you give them 100% of your attention, whenever possible. Especially in service industries.

Remember this: your customer believes they are the only customer you have. Treat everyone like they are your most important customer.

Remember Names

'Names are the sweetest and most important sound in any language.' — Dale Carnegie.

One of the easiest, simplest ways to get into rapport with another person is to use their name. It makes the meeting personal straight away. People love to think that they have made an impression on you and that you have remembered them. Personally, if someone forgets my name, I feel I am not important to them.

I have had two bosses that were brilliant at this. Even though they encountered a huge amount of people. They were two of the best bosses I ever had.

But I know people find this hard.

ACTIVATE RAS YOUR

Start by telling yourself that you are brilliant at remembering names. This will activate your brain to become good at it.

When someone tells me they struggle with this, it is because they have simply not put in the effort to become good at it.

When you meet someone for the first time, mention their name as many times as possible during your first conversation.

Try to make it memorable. One trick I use is to relate their name to another person I know with the same name, or better still, a famous person. For example, Jamie – I think Jamie Oliver. It needs to be something that prompts you to remember their name next time you see them.

Of course, you would like this to be reciprocated. My tip here is to say your name twice when you introduce yourself.

'My name is Julie, Julie Monks.'

There was a standing joke among my team members who frequently referred to me as 'Julie. Julie.'

Make your own mind up about others.

This is a mistake that I have repeated many times, always to my detriment. Especially in the workplace. It is important to form your own opinions about people you meet, whether in the workplace or in a social setting.

It's hard to ignore other people's assessment of someone and it is possible that they are sharing this information as a warning. Whilst it may be wise to take a warning into account, it is far better to form your own judgment of people based on how they treat you.

Keep an open mind and form your own point of view. Just because someone else has a poor relationship with someone does not mean the same will apply to you.

Remember, we all see the world through our own eyes based on our values and our personal experience. I recall several occasions when I got off on the wrong foot with a new contact, based on what others told me. This created unnecessary animosity and uncomfortable circumstances.

Remember, people will eventually reveal their true selves to you; your job is to give them a chance to show you who they truly are.

The same goes for other people's arguments, including family!

I know this can be hard sometimes, especially when it is someone close to you and you feel the need to be on side with them. It is good to listen and empathise with their situation, but acting on their behalf may not end well! Beware of falling into the trap of getting into an argument on someone else's behalf unless that person is a young child or a vulnerable individual at risk of being bullied, which is a whole different ball game.

Be like a cat.

I am more of a dog person than a cat lady, yet I find cat behaviour interesting.

We frequently chase after things we want. In business, this is often a new customer. I was always told to relax and not to come across as too desperate.

As an enthusiastic person, I found this extremely hard, especially when new to the world of sales and recruiting. I know for sure that I scared many a prospect away with my desperation; by trying too hard to persuade them I had a fantastic opportunity for them.

Then Diana Vickers, one of my mentors, told me that if you chase something too hard, it usually runs away. This made me think about cats and dogs. When I did my demos in customer's houses, I could guarantee that if there was a cat in the house, it would walk right up to the only person in the room who was not keen on cats and calmly jump on their lap.

Yet if you are trying to chase a dog, especially a puppy; or a toddler, they will run away from you as fast as they can. The key with anything is to be more relaxed in your approach, however much you want the thing you are chasing.

If someone else has a great idea -compliment, implement and improve

Some of the most successful people in business did not invent their product; they found someone else's idea and improved on it.

James Dyson did not invent the vacuum cleaner, yet he made a product that challenged the market leader and became the most well-known name in the vacuum business.

Richard Branson did not invent low-cost trans-Atlantic flights; Freddy Laker did that! Branson took the idea and did it better. He also used the lessons learned from the failure of SkyTrain to make a success of Virgin Atlantic.

Surprisingly, Walt Disney did not invent cartoons!

We waste so much time searching for that elusive, original idea when all we need to do is improve on one that already exists.

Not every successful business needs a brand new, innovative idea to become a success. In fact, this belief can be a hurdle that may prevent you from even getting started with your business.

A few things to consider.

You are unique and will bring a different slant to any idea.

The first version of anything is not always the best. I am not giving you licence to plagiarise another business. What I am saying is that if you wanted to set up a coaching business, for example, (I am speaking to myself here I think), the fact that there seem to be so many others out there doing the same thing does not prove that the market for coaching is saturated.

If you have a yen to start your own business, you owe it to yourself to at least explore the possibilities.

Give Credit where it is due.

In the past, I have had friends who have copied the things I have done. If this happens, we should take it as a massive compliment. It is a natural progression of some friendships, as we are influenced by the people we spend the most time with.

Where this can rankle is when your idea gets passed off as being theirs and not yours. This is especially irritating in a work situation and has happened to me occasionally. I have a great idea or strategy and the boss, or a colleague, has passed it off as their idea without giving me the credit.

Most people love praise and there is nothing better than when you receive compliments.

Take My Advice

If the idea comes from someone else, give them the best compliment ever and praise them for their great concept.

Catch people doing something right

When I worked in party plan, I showcased my cosmetic products by holding a demonstration in other people's homes. There would normally be an average of eight guests attending. Anyone who has been in that line of business will know that although it can be very rewarding, the demo can be very challenging.

Inevitably, there was always one person in the room who was determined, for whatever reason, to disrupt the spiel, criticise the products, or just be downright rude.

When I got home, I would report back to my husband about how the party had gone. Despite seven of the people at the party being completely amazing, I would spend most of my time talking about the disruptive or rude one!

It is such an easy habit to fall into.

Imagine; you are having an amazing day out somewhere, like the wildlife park, for instance. There you are enjoying looking at all the different animals, loving the scenery and being out in the fresh air, with great people. Then you call into the cafe for a quick coffee and the service is bad, or it is very expensive. We feel annoyed and start moaning. Later, when people ask us about the experience, the first thing we will tell them about is how bad the cafe was.

Just talking about the bad bit of the day affects our energy negatively, marring the memory of what was otherwise an amazing day.

Similarly, we can fall into the trap of ignoring all the good things about people we interact with, complaining about the bad things they do or even criticising them for one bad thing they have done.

A friend of mine was having a great birthday. Her husband had gone to a lot of trouble; arranging lots of lovely surprises and beautiful little gifts given at intervals throughout the day. Yet somehow, they ended up having a massive row because of one little thing he did wrong. Something so insignificant that I cannot even remember what it was, and I bet she can't either!

We make the mistake of letting bad things overshadow the good. Not only does this make the other person feel bad, but it affects us negatively, too.

If you want to change someone's behaviour for the better, remember that constant criticism will have the opposite effect.

My friend Carolyn Passey gave me the best advice 'Try to catch people doing something right!'

Rather than looking for something to criticise. In relationships at work, with your children and customers. People react much better to praise than they do to criticism.

At one seminar I attended, the speaker told us, 'If you are going to criticise someone, then you should use a ratio of 5:1 praise to criticism'. This was also brilliant advice. I have been using this ever since and it has made an amazing difference to all my relationships.

The other tip I gained was that when you first greet someone, even someone you live with or see every day; give them 4 minutes of undivided attention, and really listen to them. Another friend, Linda Emmott, coined the phrase 'Four Minutes of Fabulous!'

I am taking my own advice and giving name checks to all my wise friends who have unknowingly contributed to this book! – Julie

Work with the willing

This applies especially in networking or social selling, where you need to build teams of independent ambassadors.

The CEO of a company once asked me what my strategy was for working with people who were not engaged in the business. How did I get them interested? He was a bit surprised at my answer.

'F*%$ them John,' I said, 'Work with the willing.'

I am not talking about people who lack skill or enthusiasm - we can always train and infuse those qualities. I am talking about the team member or employee who does not want to work, no matter how much you reward them, train them, or try to motivate them. They will always find an excuse, something to complain about, or someone else to blame for their lack of success. They may have the skill, but they definitely lack the will.

In the past, I wasted time and money trying to motivate and enthuse the unwilling. I felt I was constantly telling some people in my team how to get business and chasing them to follow up leads I had given them, only to find they either did not return my calls or they had not done what they said they would.

Some consultants would even sign up and take a kit; then I would never hear from them again. We used to call that 'going into witness protection' or label them 'kit-nappers.' In the early days, I spent way too much time chasing and following up people who were neither willing nor enthusiastic about building a business.

It created so much stress, and it meant that while I was wasting time doing that, I was neglecting team members who were performing well; those who genuinely wanted to build a successful business but just needed a little help or motivation from me.

I changed my strategy in a few ways. First, when signing them up, I made sure that I knew their reasons for joining the company. I discovered their 'WHY.' I also asked how much time they were prepared to dedicate to achieving their goals; and I let them know what I expected of them and what support they could expect from me in return.

It was a case of managing expectations; theirs and mine. We worked out a plan of action from day one and I made sure they had all the tools and literature they needed to get started.

I always had weekly training for new starters scheduled in my diary and invited them to attend. Additionally, we set monthly team meeting dates a year in advance and I informed them that these meetings were for their benefit. They were told they were to call me once a week for a coaching session and that this was non-negotiable, as my job was to support them.

I had a mantra; 3 strikes and you're out. This meant that if they did not call me, I would try to call them 3 times. If they did not return my calls then, I would not call them again. I would just send my weekly newsletter.

I made a point of rewarding consistent action as well as recognising successes and marking every small milestone. We set team goals, and personal goals, and I encouraged all team members to support and cheer each other along.

It's interesting to note that 20% of your team typically accomplishes 80% of the work, a concept known as the Plato

Principle. Therefore, it makes sense to spend 80% of your allocated time working with the more productive 20%

The other thing I learned was the importance of constantly recruiting new people. People's circumstances change. They may leave the business or no longer have enough time to dedicate to it. It is easier to work with new enthusiastic people than it is to motivate people who have lost interest.

Whatever business you are in, it is prudent to ask yourself these questions.

- Is this task growing my business?

- Is this action bringing in the desired results?

Final Word

Be the best you can be.

Sometimes needs must, and it is necessary for us to take a job simply because we need to earn money. We all have bills to pay, and handbags to buy!

There is nothing worse than being stuck in a job you hate and dreading going to work every day.

Over the years, I have received sound advice from my mentors. Starting with my mum, who told me that whatever job I chose, I should always strive to be the best at it I could be.

My previous jobs include a stint working in a bar work, cleaning and measuring paint thickness! Armed with this 'be the best attitude' means that I found them all enjoyable.

Whatever job you do, you have a significant role to play. The line 'work like you don't need the money' springs to mind. You owe it to yourself to make your work enjoyable and give it your best effort.

Chapter Six

Money

Money talks...what is yours saying?

*I*MPORTANT

Before tackling this important subject, I need to remind you all that I am not a financial expert! The advice I am giving here comes from years of my personal experience but should not replace advice from a qualified and registered professional financial advisor.

If you are struggling financially, you can find details of organisations that can help you here:

https://www.gov.uk/debt-advice

Speculate to accumulate

Look after the pennies and the pounds will look after themselves

Funny how many of the stock phrases we use often contradict each other.

As a seasoned people-watcher, I have often marvelled at how some people have a nice lifestyle and accumulate savings, with a relatively low income.

But then, other people, with a higher income, from better paid jobs or who have received sizeable sums of money through inheritance or redundancy, for example, seem to struggle with the old 'more month than money' chestnut.

There are always people who rush out and spend most of their months' pay in the first few days after payday, only to struggle for the rest of the month, worrying about how they are going to find enough money to pay their essential bills.

More month than money is a habit, not a fact

My generation had less to spend their money on than today's millennials. Mobile phones and gaming centres were not a thing when I was a teenager. I spent my early working life learning a trade, specifically hairdressing, and saving for my first car and then a house.

I was lucky; my parents taught me the importance of saving money. I am grateful for that lesson, but my parents' money mentality revolved around scarcity. My mother shunned any kind of materialism and brought me up to believe that we would always be poor; that we did not deserve better. There was never money for luxuries.

But I wanted more. I wanted a big, clean, lovely house and a nice car to drive. I chose not to follow my parent's example.

Both my parents worked, which meant I was cared for by childminders. This turned out to be a blessing for me, as it exposed me to different ways of living and looking at life. I am especially grateful for the lessons those families taught me, good and bad.

Money is not only a piece of paper or a number on a bank statement. It is the energy and feelings you attach to it that matter. Some people believe you must work hard for money and that it is hard to accumulate, while others seem to attract money with ease.

What are your thoughts and feelings about money?

Grab a piece of paper and ask yourself the following questions:

There are no right or wrong answers here. This exercise is for you to explore your relationship with money.

- Does having money make you feel happy?
- Does having money help you feel secure?
- Do you feel stressed about your lack of money?
- Does having money or a lack of it affect your status?
- Do you feel you have enough money for your needs?
- Do you feel you lack money?
- Do you spend money freely with no thought about the consequences?
- When you make a new purchase, how do you feel afterwards, i.e., Guilty? Happy?
- Do you feel in control of your finances?
- How do you feel when bills arrive?

- Do you believe you deserve to be rich?
- Do you feel destined to be poor?
- Does money equal success in your mind?
- How is your bank balance?

What have you learned from this exercise about your money mindset?

Was your energy affected negatively or positively by each question?

Your perception of money is key to how you generate more and utilise what you have more effectively.

There have been many books written about accumulating and keeping more money. The aim of this chapter is to share the lessons I have learned through personal experience and research.

Money mind-set

How often do you think about money?

It's been said that the poor spend more time thinking about money, or the lack of it, than the rich.

Once I changed my beliefs, my focus, and my energy around the subject of money, my finances improved. Lots of us have been programmed to believe that we will never have or keep money. Or even that we do not deserve lots of money.

Think back to the language you heard when you were growing up. Was it positive or negative?

This is often the key to your relationship with money.

Did you constantly hear phrases like 'Money doesn't grow on trees' or 'We can't afford it'?

Or were your parents/guardians always stating the cost of things?

Were you taught that the only way to receive money was to earn it and that accumulating it any other way was a sin?

Have you been conditioned to believe that money is a bad thing? *Note, this is something that you may not be consciously aware of.*

If any of these things apply to you, then subconsciously you will always find ways of getting rid of your money. This is one of the main reasons that lottery winners are offered lots of financial advice as soon as they claim their winnings.

So, what changed for me?

After reading a few books on the subject, I decided I was deserving of money. I realised that the story I had been told during my formative years, about always being destined to be poor, was not set in stone. Also, having money or not would not change who I was as a person, but it could change my circumstances.

It was ok to aspire to a different life than the one my parents had expected me to lead. I did not have to feel guilty about desiring to be wealthy or having a more luxurious lifestyle than my parents. Also, I had been conditioned to believe that earning money required huge effort.

Once I had grasped the idea that it was perfectly fine for money to flow to me easily and I had an expectation that it would, my life changed for the better. I found I could focus on the tasks that would grow my business and relax about the outcome.

With this new money mindset, my income grew 10 times within 8 months. With more money available to spend, I soon developed a serious designer bag and shoes habit! But it was a little while before I could enjoy spending it on myself without feeling guilty about the fact that I was splashing out on little luxuries for myself.

Then I had the idea of allowing myself to indulge or reward myself by spending 10% of my commission cheque. This removed the guilt and ensured that I was sensible with the rest of it.

I allocated a further 10% to investments that I would never touch; 10% went into an easy-access savings account; and the remaining 70% used for general life.

One of the most important lessons I learned from reading self-development books was that rich people prioritise saving and then spend what is left, while poor people prioritise spending and then attempt to save what is left. Inevitably, they did not have any money left at the end of the month. Or worse still, they ended up living on their overdraft or borrowing money to get through.

To summarise:

- *10% To spend on me*
- *10% Long-term Investments*
- *10% Easy access savings*
- *70% General life*

Recently, I had an interesting conversation with my stepdaughter on this subject. Her parents had separated, and this meant that she had very conflicting influences around money. One very frugal parent, always stating the cost of things, telling her that money had to be earned to get the things that you wanted/needed. Whereas the other parent constantly splashed out on luxuries and experiences.

On the one hand, she received encouragement to earn and save extra cash, but she also experienced an 'easy come, easy go' attitude towards money.

My take on her situation was that she had learned good lessons from both parents. She knew about budgeting and the importance of working to earn her money, and luckily, this was the example she had taken on board. But she also learned that money equals freedom.

I started teaching my grandchildren about money when they were around six years old. I used to give them £1 pocket money when I picked them up from school once a week. Then I would ask them; 'Spend or save?'

I set them a goal of saving £20 with no time limit. When they achieved the target, I would give them £5 in interest. Of course, the bank of Nanna pays top rates of interest compared to the corporate banking world!

I also gave them the option of spending some and saving the rest. They enjoyed the exercise and learned a small lesson about unearned income.

Managing your finances

At the time of writing, the UK is in the middle of a cost-of-living crisis - according to the media.

One of the joys of adulthood is the need to pay the bills. I have been in a position, both personally and in business, where I have struggled to do this. I have also met many people who are in a debt crisis. Sometimes not of their own making, sometimes because of poor money management skills.

At the beginning of the chapter, I told you that my parents taught me all this at a very young age. Good advice, which I must admit, I ignored - until I got into trouble with money. A common mistake!

Unmanageable debt is detrimental to your mental health and your financial health.

3 of the most common causes of debt are:

- Poor budgeting

- Overspending

- Not keeping abreast of your financial situation

I have witnessed this so many times. Payday comes and people splash out! Spending on luxuries and little treats as soon as the money lands in their bank account.

'Well, I've worked hard all month, so I've earned a treat or two or three...' they tell themselves.

Then, for the rest of the month, they struggle to find the money for basics. And if an unforeseen circumstance crops up, they do not have any reserves to pay for it.

Living 'hand to mouth.'

Usually, there is no need to live this way.

Basic budgeting

> *'You must gain control over your money or the lack of it will forever control you.'* - Dave Ramsey

Run your personal finances as you would run a business

Any successful business has good cash flow management. Knowing exactly what is due in and out is vital to any business, and it is also vital to you and your peace of mind. Look after your personal finances in the same way.

- Calculate your basic bills, bearing in mind that the most important will be your rent or mortgage payment.
- Include utilities, loans, and other regular payments.
- Allow for spending on food and basics.
- What do you have left?
- What are your outgoings versus your income?
- Are you spending more than you are bringing in?
- What can you do to redress the balance?
- Ideally, dedicate a regular amount to savings

In his book The Richest Man in Babylon, George S Clason recommends you save 10% of your income as you can survive on the other 90%. (This 1926 book is still in print, so it seems like he knew what he was talking about!)

Once you pay your bills and set aside 10%, you can choose to do whatever you like with the remaining amount. It is that simple.

Need to make some savings?

Check what you are paying out. It is surprising how all those little spends add up.

- Keep a grip on your subscriptions. Are they essential? How much are they costing? -

- Are you paying for a gym membership and not going regularly?

- How often are you eating out or ordering takeaway? Could you cut this down and cook at home?

The intention is not to deprive you of everything you enjoy. By eliminating unnecessary expenses, you can live as joyful a life as possible.

Overspending

Face it: if you are spending more than you are bringing in, you are unlikely to catch up, unless you have a guaranteed promotion in the next few months. Simple maths will tell you that even if you spend just a little more than your income, the compound effect will increase your debt each month. In addition, if you are using credit to cope, then interest due will increase your debt exponentially.

People often feel tempted to take out a consolidation loan to include all their debts. This is one solution, as most bank loans offer fixed interest rates. But beware! Too often, I have witnessed the downside of this solution. Once you clear the credit card, it is easy to allow the debt to build up again, leaving you in the same situation as before, with the additional problem of needing to pay off the loan.

Do you *need* it, or do you *want* it?

When I think about it, I have probably made around £250,000 worth of financial mistakes during my 40-odd years as an adult. Thank goodness I have made more good financial decisions than bad ones. Spending money is easy! Many people spend much more than they have.

When we are spending money on luxuries, we are chasing a feeling. Looking back, I have probably spent far too much on shoes, bags, and clothing. That is fine if you can afford it.

The thrill you get when you purchase a new item never lasts for long. It wears off soon after the purchase. I know many people who own lots of items they have never used whose wardrobes are stuffed full of clothes they have never worn.

My personal downfall came while I was working in direct sales. I was required to attend lots of conferences and enjoyed regular incentive trips. I had this stupid idea that I needed a new wardrobe of clothes for every event because I didn't want to be seen in the same outfit too often.

Looking back now, it seems ridiculous!

What I was trying to buy was not lots of new clothes; it was the feeling of confidence that I felt each new outfit would give me.

Many of the things we buy are based on feelings, including status items like expensive cars and those designer clothes and handbags. All fine if the cost is within your means. But it becomes a problem when you need to stretch your finances to accommodate this type of spending.

Take My Advice

When you feel tempted to make a luxury purchase, ask yourself; do I *need* this item, or do I *want* this item? If in doubt, leave it out.

Wait at least 24 hours- Do you still want it as much?

If it is an item of clothing, does it match at least 3 other things in your current wardrobe? Where will you wear this item? If it is for an event – do you have anything already that would be suitable and that you will feel good wearing?

Now if buying clothes, my rule of thumb is; if I spend time in front of the mirror, twisting and turning, trying to find a position that will make the item suit me, then I probably won't like it much in the future!

It will either end up in the charity shop or being sold on Vinted for a mere fraction of the purchase price.

Unless I feel instantly good wearing it, I do not purchase it.

If it is a big purchase, such as a car, steer away from making an impulse buy.

It is easy to get caught up with the ambience of the showroom and the sales spiel. Before you know it, you have signed up for a finance deal and are spending far more than you intended over a long period. Far better to do some research first. Work out how much you can afford to spend on the monthly payments and check the deposit you need if you are intending to buy on finance.

Check the cost of motor insurance and road tax too.

Think about things that might catch you out in the future, such as maintenance and new tyres. How much will a warranty cost you? All these little extras can add up and will end up tipping the balance of your finances.

- What will be the secondary gain of buying a status car?
- What is the feeling you are chasing?
- What would it mean to you if you were to go for a lower-status car or item which was within your budget?

I understand that ownership of these things can bring with it a great feeling. So, if it is within your means, then enjoy the purchase.

If you do not have the funds but still crave that beautiful high-status item, don't give up on the idea. Set a savings goal to finance the purchase.

This could include finding a side hustle to bring more money in.

Keeping control

People's financial problems are often simply the result of them ignoring the warning signs.

People end up in a much worse situation because they have buried their heads in the sand. Refusing to deal with bills and avoiding opening debt letters. As a result, they end up in even bigger debt by incurring fines, surcharges, and interest payments.

A prime example of this is the £60 parking fine, which is ignored and ends up costing thousands of pounds. Or may even bring the bailiffs to your door.

These dire situations can usually be avoided if you deal with them promptly. The more you avoid the problem, the worse it becomes for your mental well-being.

Not dealing with your situation will not make the problems magically disappear, it will only exacerbate them further.

Take My advice

'Feel the fear and do it anyway' - Susan Jeffries

- Open that letter or email immediately.
- If you really cannot afford to pay the fine or the missed

payment penalty charge, contact the company involved as soon as you can. Let them know your current situation and see if they can either waive the extra charges or set up an affordable payment plan. Credit card companies will often waive the late payment charge if your previous payments have been up to date.

- If, despite everything, you find you are still struggling, perhaps following a change of circumstances, then inform your debtors as soon as possible rather than allowing things to escalate.

- In the long run, the outcome will be better if you take control of the situation, rather than waiting until your debtors contact you.

There are many organisations that can help you with debt management. Do not be afraid to ask for help. You can get free, confidential and independent advice on dealing with debt problems here: https://www.gov.uk/debt-advice

Pay your bills on time.

- Always make a point of paying your bills on time. This goes hand in hand with basic budgeting. Nowadays, we have instant access to our bank accounts, and this means it is much easier to keep abreast of your finances.

- Set up direct debits for all your regular payments. But remember, it is very important to ensure there are funds in your account for when they become due. I set up my direct debits for a few days after I get paid, so they don't surprise me at the end of the month.

- If you have been accurate in your budget calculation, then there should always be money to pay your direct debits.

- Remember to allow for unexpected extras like the interest on credit cards.

Pay your bills with gratitude

I am extremely grateful that we have always had enough money for our needs.

I learned about money gratitude from reading The Magic. A book from Rhonda Byrne's The Secret series.

- Are you grateful that you can pay your bills?

- Or do you worry about how you are going to pay them?

- How do you feel when they arrive in your inbox or on your doormat?

I learned to imagine that every bill was a cheque rather than a bill. Every time I pay a bill I write 'Thank you. Paid' on it.

The more grateful you are for the money you have, then the more money you will attract.

Managing and utilising credit

Despite all the drawbacks, there will always be times when it is useful to use a credit card.

But this comes with a **massive warning!**

If you are already in debt or you have got into trouble in the past, then stay away from the plastic.

There are advantages to credit cards but let me stress again; you need to be in tight control of your money situation before you utilise them.

Occasionally, it is beneficial to use them. For instance, if you are making a large purchase or travelling abroad. Using a credit card will ensure you have better purchase protection.

Take My Advice

If you are using a credit card regularly for online purchases, factor this into your monthly budget and make sure you have the funds to clear the statement balance at the end of the month.

- If you are going to use them for 'extras' like Christmas spending or a holiday, then you must factor in the monthly repayments into your budget and be sure to allow for the interest charged.

- Make the payments on time to avoid late payment charges.

- Having a credit card and paying your bill on time increases your credit score and the amount of credit available to you.

- Beware of store cards and catalogues, as their interest rates are much higher.

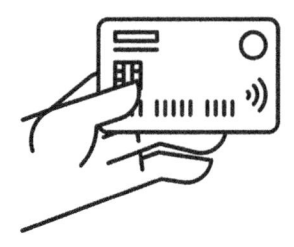

Getting back in control of your credit card balances

Credit cards can be your friend or your foe. It all depends how you use them.

People frequently get into an awful mess with them.

While I am no money expert, I have had form in the past! I feel compelled to share my tips on this subject with you as they come from personal experience.

With the current financial crisis here in the UK, many people are relying on credit cards for everyday expenses, rather than keeping them for emergency spending. Credit cards are an expensive way to borrow money, and recent interest rate hikes have left people struggling to keep on top of their repayments.

If you find yourself in the position where you cannot meet payments due, contact the credit card company as soon as possible. They may reduce the interest or even freeze it and can help you set up an affordable repayment plan.

Another option is to see if you can transfer the balance onto an interest free card. But check that the transfer fee is lower than the interest you would have been paying.

Remember that if you miss a payment, you will incur a late payment charge which adds to the debt and extra interest.

As I mentioned before, another option that may help if you are struggling with debt is to take out a consolidation bank loan to cover all your outstanding card balances. This may not be an option if you have a poor credit record. Remember, loan payments are not as flexible as credit payments.

Although if you are struggling, this can be an advantage.

There is a downside to this. Having your card balances cleared with one manageable monthly payment going out may be a relief, but you may still be tempted to use the remaining credit on the cards. Don't do it! It could leave you in a much worse position.

If you would like a copy of my managing your credit card and clearing your balances worksheet, please email info@julie-monks.co.uk

Never a borrower or a lender be

> 'Before borrowing money from a friend, decide which you need most.' Joe Moore

One of the quickest ways to end a friendship is to either lend or borrow money.

Lending

Something else I have first-hand experience of. There have been several occasions when I have lent someone money and they have never returned it to me. I guess I am an optimistic fool. Pestering them for repayment failed. In one instance, they moved away without telling me or making any attempt to pay me back. This left me with a bad feeling for a long time. Testing my faith in humanity.

Borrowing

Even the best of us can be over-optimistic when it comes to borrowing money, believing we will pay it back. If you are considering borrowing money from people, particularly friends or family, my advice is to avoid it if possible. Unless you can guarantee 100% that you will pay them back within the agreed time frame. It is the same situation as lending, only reversed. The quickest way to cause friction is if you don't pay it back on time or do not repay it at all.

Take my advice

If you are going to lend someone money, do it. But with the expectation it is possible that you will never get it back. This applies especially when lending to a family member.

- If it will leave you short of money and cause you a problem if you do not pay it back within a certain time frame, then I urge you not to do it.

- I *always* feel uncomfortable asking for it back.

- Do not borrow from friends or family unless you are sure you can pay it back.

Summary

- What did you discover from answering the money mindset questions?

- What are you going to change about your relationship with money?

- Save 10% of your income; you can learn to survive on the other 90%.

- Run your personal finances as you would run a business.

- Control your cash flow.

- Use basic budgeting to help you keep control of your income and expenditure.

- Pause before you buy a luxury item; is it a want or a need?

- If you are getting into difficulties or struggling to make payments, take control.

- Always pay your bills on time and with gratitude.

- If you must use credit cards, keep a firm grip on how much you borrow and the repayments.

- Never borrow from or lend to family and friends.

- Seek expert advice when necessary.

Chapter Seven

Compassion over Comparison

Free yourself from the burden of comparison

The biggest critic we encounter in our lives is ourselves. We see the world from behind our own eyes. We often waste time worrying about others' opinions of us, when what we are doing is projecting our thoughts about our shortcomings onto the people we interact with. Sadly, when we compare ourselves to others, it's rarely favourably.

Here's an interesting fact I read this very morning in Brian Tracy's book 'Believe it to achieve it'. The 99-to-1 rule. This says people spend 99 per cent of their time thinking about themselves and only 1 per cent thinking about everyone else.

Comparison with others is not always a bad thing, sometimes it can be aspirational and motivate us to make a change for the better.

Seeking outside approval

It is a strange thing to admit, but in the past, I have sometimes felt that other people don't like me; that they disapprove of me; that I do not fit in.

I expect some of you have had a similar experience.

My father was an immigrant, and my mother worked full time. This set me apart from the other children I knew.

Or it could have been because I was a scruffy child with a squint! Who knows?

I have much to thank those people for. It inspired me to want something better for myself and my future family.

Those feelings stayed with me until recently, when I decided it was time to exorcise them once and for all. By exploring whose voice I was hearing in my head when seeking to impress; or which voices made me afraid to try something because of fear of ridicule.

Take My Advice

Here is the simple exercise I devised.

Start without delving too deeply into your memory; you don't need all that crap in your brain

Write an Approval / Disapproval list

Under the heading Disapproval: Think of all the people who you felt disapproved of you in the past; you do not need to remember all of them, only the people whose comments or disapproval significantly impacted you negatively.

Make a list; if you cannot remember their names, identify them in some other way. For instance, the way you met them, e.g., Lady who was on playground duty at my first school.

Now under the heading Approval: List all the people who have given you positive reactions or feedback.

Compare the lists

This was an incredible exercise for me! I wish I had done it 40 years ago.

Significant Disapproval List: 7

Approval List: 100 and counting...

What an eye-opener!

The first list was small and most of the people on it had not figured in my life for years.

I took this opportunity to thank them for driving me to improve my life dramatically; then I let those feelings go. I stopped doubting myself based on how people I can hardly remember, none of whom have become famous for their significant achievements, made me feel.

I bet you can do the same!

Befriend yourself

We are our own worst critic, expert at berating ourselves over minor details, which only serves to make us feel even worse than we do already.

Tackle this by stepping away from your own persona and treating yourself as you would a close friend or child; someone you care about and want the best outcome for.

What would you say to them in the same situation?

I am sure you would find words of reassurance or offer some brilliant advice.

When people brag to you, take it as a compliment

Imagine that you are talking to someone who starts bragging about their life. How do you feel?

It could be about everything and anything. All their wonderful possessions; how amazing they are at their job and everything they do; or how incredible their family is.

When we are in comparison mode, this creates feelings of inadequacy. We may even actively dislike the person doing the bragging in that moment.

Then one day it occurred to me that there might be another reason for them making such an effort to impress me. Instead of assuming they are playing the game of one-upmanship, consider that are hoping to impress you because they think you are worth impressing. So, take it as a massive compliment! Enjoy the interaction and feel confident about yourself.

Compliments and criticism

There is a fine line between a spiteful comment and constructive criticism.

How come we receive nine compliments and only one criticism, but the thing that sticks with us, going round and round in our head, is that single adverse comment?

I am all for self-improvement and taking advice. But we need to develop a balanced approach to this. I never mind someone telling me something if they take the time to explain the benefits of their suggestion.

Similarly, if you are the person making the comment, pause before speaking. Think about what you are saying, and why:

- Do you have their best interests at heart?
- Are you genuinely offering help?
- Or are you doing it to ridicule or feel superior to the recipient?

If the last is true, then don't!

Australian body language expert, Allan Pease, says that people do things to 'avoid a pain, or to make a gain.' Pause and ask yourself, which one are you?

Next, think about how you react. Previous generations seem to have had thicker skin. They did not appear to be so easily offended by criticism or 'advice.'

Start by considering who is giving you the advice and look for evidence of their expertise in that area. Do you respect them as a person and for what they have achieved?

The truth often hurts! That is why we don't like unsolicited advice.

Comparison is the thief of joy!

When I was young, going to school and having my performance compared to others was unbearable. I always felt that I was not as good as the other people in my class; not as trendy; didn't have the right shoes, etc.

Imagine how hard it is to be a teenager now, constantly bombarded by images of 'perfection' from social media.

Now I am older, I still find it a challenge not to compare my life unfavourably to other people's perfect lives.

When my children were young, our house was more like a building site than a home. My husband was a builder, the type who would knock the whole back of the house out, and then take 13 years (yes, 13 years) to finish it. I lived in that mess all those years, buried in dust and disorganisation, with little or no storage.

The perfect white world of the washing powder adverts left me feeling totally inadequate. An impromptu visit from anyone who did not know me well caused extreme distress; I was so ashamed of the way I was living.

There is even an old English word for it.

Scurryfunge (verb) - sku-ree-fun-j – *Old English: to rush around cleaning when company is on their way over.*

Not much used nowadays, but it should be!

At the time I was running my own busy hairdressing salon and looking after my children, but I felt like a massive failure compared to my friends, who appeared able to keep immaculate houses.

It took me until my mid-fifties to stop comparing myself unfavourably to others. A chance comment from one of my delegates, Kersti Kidman, enlightened me.

'The trouble is, we are comparing how we feel on the inside to other people's outside projections,' she said.

This was a light bulb moment for me. People only reveal what they want you to see; the photoshopped, edited version of themselves.

Social media provides an easy and efficient way for people to do this. My friend used to say that Facebook was her Disney life. It would be lovely to have a superpower ability to see into other people's minds occasionally, but none of us do, so we cannot see what they are really feeling. People let you see what they want you to see and tell you what they want you to believe. Often this is about self-protection, so try not to judge them too badly.

Most of us have projected Swan syndrome at some point – you know, where we look like we are sailing smoothly along but underneath we are paddling away like crazy.

We also look for others who may not be doing as well as us in certain aspects of our lives. It might be so we can feel better about ourselves. At other times, it gives us an excuse for not achieving something.

Having a role model can be a great and productive thing, but it is no good to us if we use them as a stick to beat ourselves with.

Remember, comparing ourselves to others can make us feel bad about ourselves.

We fear the judgment of others too and worry about what they think of us. But trust me, most people are only thinking about themselves. If they are finding fault with you, it is probably because they see something in you they don't like about the way they are. Or they are looking for something to help them feel better about their life or situation.

See? Avoiding a pain or making a gain. Just stop doing it!

Ask yourself these questions.

- If nothing could stop you; if someone waved a magic wand and created a miracle, what kind of person would you like to be?

- If you could choose, how would you like to feel every day?

- What would you be doing every day?

- How would you really like to live your life?

- How can you feel at ease in your own skin?

- What is it you want to change about yourself? Hey, if you are happy as you are and feel at home in your skin, that is something to celebrate!

- What makes you feel happy and accomplished?

- How would feeling happy and accomplished make you feel?

- What immediate action do you need to take? Remember, we are all beautiful, but we are all a work in progress!

- When you meet someone, what can you learn from them? Whether it is someone you already know or someone new. Focus on enjoying your time with them in the now. This applies to work colleagues as well.

- What are they are doing to make you feel uncomfortable?

- Are they succeeding at something that you would like to succeed at?

If that is the case, ask them for their advice. Most people love sharing their ideas.

- How would it feel if you were not worrying about trying to impress them or wondering what their impression of you is?

- What are they doing that you could implement in your life?

- What are you not doing that really bugs you? I was not cooking proper meals and eating at irregular times. Easy to fix!

- Ask yourself, "Am I prepared to put the effort in to change whatever is bugging me?"

I promise you; you have the power to change how you feel about yourself.

Remember! It is OK to pat yourself on the back or toot your own horn. You are worth impressing.

Never explain!

Do you ever feel the need to make excuses for who you are or for the state of your house?

Do you hear yourself saying 'Excuse the mess,' or 'I look a mess?'

When we use phrases like this, are we fishing for a compliment? Looking to provide reassurance and build our confidence? More often, I believe it is because we are embarrassed about something.

As you know, for me, it was usually the state of my house. I was constantly saying 'Excuse the mess!' before guests even stepped inside the door, feeling the need to explain myself.

Let's be fair, a messy house is hardly a crime!

> *Although when my house is tidy, I do feel like I have my act together! – Julie*

Then I had a revelation! I was visiting a friend's house, and she had just had a new kitchen installed. I thought it was beautiful. Then she pointed out that she had not had the tiling done. 'Excuse the walls, they look terrible,' she said.

I was so busy admiring her new kitchen units that I had not even noticed the lack of tiles! That was when I realised that we rarely notice things until someone points them out to us.

Remember your RAS

From that day on I stopped drawing attention to my flaws and never ever say 'Excuse the mess.' You do not need a detailed explanation of everything. As the late Queen of England would state, 'Never explain, never complain.'

Remember, most people are more interested in themselves than you and your faults. What is the worst that can happen? They could tell someone else that you have a messy house. Is that going to harm you?

The strange thing about this phenomenon is that the most judgemental people are not happy with something in their own lives, so they relish finding someone in a worse predicament than them.

I remember one friend commenting on the state of another friend's house. I had to bite my tongue because I knew hers was in a far, far worse state.

> *Oops! There I am, sounding judgmental myself!* –
> *Julie*

Well, the title of the book is Take My Advice, I'm not using it!

We all have different priorities. My friend spends a lot of time doing lovely things with her extended family, making beautiful memories. The state of her house is not high on her list of priorities. They are one of the happiest families I know, and it is lovely to see.

Take My Advice

Everyone has different priorities!

What is important to them may not be important to you.

Conserve your energy by not comparing an apple to a pear.

There is never any good reason to highlight your shortcomings to anyone.

Chapter Eight

Dealing With Overwhelm

When it all gets too much

Now we come to one of the main reasons for me writing this book.

In the last decade, I have witnessed more and more people becoming overwhelmed with life, including myself.

Life seemed so much simpler when I was growing up. Maybe it just felt that way because I was young and had fewer responsibilities. But I think it is more than that.

Go with the flow

We all have bad days, even me sometimes! With no idea why. They come from nowhere. One minute everything is going well, and we feel on top of the world; in the vortex, as Esther Hicks would say. Then, in the blink of an eye, we are spiralling down, heading for rock bottom.

No matter how hard we work; even if we do all the things we are supposed to do. One moment we feel in flow and high on life. Then, out of nowhere, fatigue strikes, and we find ourselves re-visiting the bad habits of our past behaviour.

When this happens, it is easy to give in, revert to our old ways and waste a few more days wallowing in misery. Beating ourselves up about what we ought to be doing and feeling completely overwhelmed by all the tasks on our to-do list.

But we should remind ourselves that it is ok to have off days. There is no rule that says we must be 100% productive all the time. No one is monitoring our daily activities and judging us for how we spend our time. Unless you are working for someone else, that is!

It would be lovely if we had unlimited amounts of energy all the time. I have met people that appear to be in control of every aspect of their lives.

We are all different and different things energise us. My goal is to help you find a way that fits in with your persona, enabling you to feel more in flow with your life.

Every day is different

Just because yesterday was a bad day does not mean every day will be bad.

In the realm of self-development, people often advise us we have the power to choose how we feel each day and how we react to any situation. It is up to us. Whilst I agree with this in principle and frequently put it into practice, there are still occasions when, for no reason in particular, the day just feels wrong.

Recently, I have been doing some energy work, and that has been extremely helpful. You can read more about this in The Energy Alignment Method by Yvette Taylor.

For those of you who, like me, are not ready to delve into details and just need to hear some practical stuff, here you go:

First, some days are just that way! There simply does not seem to be any reason for it. We just feel 'down in the mouth' - as my mother would say.

Start by telling yourself that this feeling will pass. Think of it as a moment where your energy is vibrating at a lower level. For me, the temptation is to hibernate and not interact with anyone. My go-to solution is sitting in my nest, reading a book.

This works for a while, and we are constantly reminded to listen to our bodies when they tell us to rest. This is good advice, but it's also important to check in with ourselves regularly.

Ask yourself a few simple questions.

- What are you hiding from?
- Are you just tired?
- Is this resting? Or are you in overwhelm?
- Do you have that uneasy feeling that you get when you know there is an urgent task that needs completing, yet you feel unable to tackle it? Because you feel scared or something else is preventing you?

I call this the Head Fizzle feeling.

The longer you spend wallowing in a bad feeling, the worse it will feel.

Action is the answer.

Confession time – that is exactly the way I am feeling now! Which is what prompted me to write this chapter. Action IS the answer. – Julie

Of course, it is impossible to feel on top of the world and enthusiastic about life all the time. How would we know the difference if we did not have different moods? The secret to survival is to be kind to yourself; to not waste time berating yourself for feeling this way. It is good to recognise it and to explore what happened, to make you feel so lethargic or not yourself.

For me, this feeling is usually brought on by overwhelm; having to do things which I am not familiar with or find hard to implement; or dealing with something that I fear the outcome of. These things make me feel uncomfortable.

My way of dealing with this is to retreat into avoidance or distraction mode. My go-to behaviours are reading or binge-watching television. This is not necessarily a bad thing; sometimes it is our body's way of telling us to pause or rest. It can be a good thing to remove yourself from a situation for a short time and take a break. But. And it is a huge BUT. There is a very fine line between resting and resetting and falling into a depressive state.

If this happens, set yourself a time limit of 24 hours to wallow.

If you really cannot get out of your own head, try getting how you are feeling down on paper. It is amazing how quickly this can clear your mind and lift your mood.

Start with just one small task, one you know you can accomplish with ease.

Ask yourself.

- What is *making my head fizz?*
- What is making me feel uncomfortable?
- What should I be doing that is making me feel uneasy?

Are you suffering with Head Fizzle?

We all have times when we feel overwhelmed by everything on our to-do list; even more so when the list is so long, we do not know where to begin. We end up burying our heads in the sand in full ostrich mode, in dire need of a lolling day.

When you find yourself in overwhelm it feels as though you have an internal washing machine going around in your stomach and your head simultaneously. Take a pause and think deeply about which task is disrupting your mind.

Which scenario keeps whirring around in your consciousness? Which task do you keep putting off, the one that you are imagining yourself doing repeatedly?

Remember, the brain does not know the difference between thinking and doing, so just imagining the task will leave you feeling exhausted.

Once you have identified which task is causing the problem, get it done before you do anything else.

Because once you have sorted it, you will find the blockage, eliminate that stuck feeling, and all your other tasks will feel much easier to do. The bonus feeling is one of achievement and relief.

If you really cannot face a tricky or scary task, try this; set a timer for 25 minutes and commit to completing the job within that time. If you cannot get to grips with it in the allocated time, then you can attempt it another day.

I can guarantee that the hardest part is getting started; after 25 minutes, you will want to get on and finish the job.

Top tip 1:

If it is a long task, when the 25 minutes are up, take a five-minute break and then start the timer for another 25 minutes. Keep repeating the process until you are done. It is amazing how much you can achieve in a short space of time when you focus. This method of time management is known as the Pomodoro technique.

Top tip 2:

Apply the 'Always do the hardest task first' rule. You will find all the following tasks are much easier to complete, and your day will flow. I recommend reading the book Eat That Frog by Brian Tracy. It is short and to the point.

Action really is the answer, and small actions lead to bigger actions. Once you are in motion and have completed one task, even a ridiculously small one, you will find it easier to face tackling some of the harder ones on your list.

My strategy is to move to the head i job as soon as possible. They are probably the ones blocking your day and making you feel uneasy.

Things are much easier than we imagine. The secret is to get started. Sometimes you just need to step on the pedal and go!

What is that one thing you simply do not want to do? If it is possible, go do it right this second. Tell yourself,

'I will do it for 25 minutes and see how it goes. If I really cannot get into it, then I will stop for now.'

It is amazing how good it feels to get started.

Starting the job activates the enthusiasm to complete it.

I have a friend who needs to lose weight for health reasons. Her favourite phrase is, 'I am going to start the diet once I lose half a stone.' This sounds like absolute madness to me, and she has been saying this for the last two years!

Are you one of those Monday morning or New Year's resolution people? Do you tell yourself that you need to be in the right frame of mind before you can start something, whether it is a new business or a new fitness routine?

I love that feeling of being fired up and enthusiastic about something. I enjoy setting up a new business, discovering a new hobby, or even getting involved in starting small things, such as running a committee.

We mistakenly believe that we constantly need to feel the exhilaration of being in flow. Often, the opposite is true. We sit and wait for circumstances to be ideal, hoping the planets will align to create the perfect opportunity. All we are doing is wasting time, putting off doing the things that could make a positive difference in our lives.

Why wait till Monday? Next month? A new year?

All we need to do is take the first step. With each forward movement, each small bit of progress, our enthusiasm grows and becomes more sustainable.

Fears

> *'Many times, the thought of fear itself is greater than what it is we fear.'* – Idowu Koyenikan, *Wealth for All: Living a Life of Success at the Edge of Your Ability*

Fear holds us back from making progress.

For example:

- We think we are going to fail.
- We fear being ridiculed.
- We are afraid that we will not live up to other people's expectations.
- We are afraid that we won't live up to our own expectations.
- We hate saying we are going to achieve something and then not doing so.

I have a great phrase on my desktop mood maker that says.

> 'DO NOT EXPECT TO FEEL
> THE HEAT UNTIL
> YOU THROW ON SOME LOGS.'

Another quote I love:

> *'The person who never makes a mistake will never make anything.'* - Theodore Roosevelt

There is a reason behind these feelings. Our brain is programmed to keep us safe. *Not to keep us happy.* It works on the premise that what we know, what we are familiar with, will keep us safe. This explains why people stay too long in jobs they hate or remain with abusive partners.

The good news is - we have the power to change this. Our brain is always creating new neurological pathways - whatever our age.

Let's explore fear of failure.

> *Failure is the scenery on the road to success* – Julie Monks

It is ok to fail.

The more we fail, the better we get at things. A baby does not simply wake up one day and start walking. It takes practice. Trial and error.

I have watched so many people live miserable lives because they were too afraid to fail or make a mistake.

My Mother was a prime example. She rarely did anything that took her out of her comfort zone. If she feared it, then she never attempted it.

For me, 'what ifs' are far more damaging than 'I tried, but I failed.' It is always better to give it a go.

My decision to write this book is a splendid example. If it turns out to be a failure, and nobody reads it, at least I have the satisfaction that I gave it a shot!

Wanting to try something but being paralysed by a fear of failure is the worst feeling. The idea spins round and round in our heads, and we make bargains with ourselves to justify our lack of action:

- I will write the book when my office is tidy.

- I will join the gym when I have lost a stone.

- I will start cooking healthy meals when I have a new kitchen.

- I will make the sales calls when it is the right time of day. (Which incidentally seems to be never).

- I will do such-and-such when I have more time.

One of my jobs was credit control for our structural steel painting company. We had a horrible and rude customer who I hated calling. He always tried to get out of paying. I would put off calling him. I told myself it was not much money anyway and if I waited a while longer, he would pay up

But here's the thing! When I did finally pick up the phone and call him, I always felt better. Irrespective of if he paid us or not!

Here's why. Our body/nervous system does not know the difference between thinking about something and doing it.

Visualise yourself sucking a juicy wedge of lemon. Imagine all the sharp juices dripping onto your tongue. 95% of you are salivating right now!

This is evidence that the body cannot differentiate between what you are thinking about and the action you are taking.

What have I learned from this?

Just step on the pedal and do it!

Whether you physically do something or only think about doing it, you will experience the same amount of fear. I usually find that getting the task done causes me less anxiety than all my thinking about it. It takes up less time too.

Take my advice

A great little tip for when you feel afraid. Tell yourself that you are excited rather than anxious. A good example of this for me is the ironing pile, probably because it is so visual.

It sits there, taunting you. I used to hide it away in a cupboard so that it was not visible. But out of sight was not out of mind. I constantly thought about tackling it and became increasingly anxious about it. I had all the worry and stress about it, but without the reward and satisfaction of seeing it completed.

No wonder I felt constantly exhausted and guilty if I tried to relax, having *not* done it.

This was total madness! Once I started the job, I found it quite enjoyable. Seeing neatly folded piles of freshly ironed clothes always gives me great satisfaction.

Release the feeling of obligation to anything - clothes people, events, things, or the promises you have made yourself.

Even though I am constantly clearing out and decluttering, I am amazed at the amount of crappy stuff I still own. My advice is to avoid buying it in the first place!

Another piece of my advice that I seem to have ignored!
– Julie

I left my parents' home over 40 years ago. All I took with me were my clothes and a few odd things I had saved in my 'bottom drawer' (something we did in the old days to prepare for married life – even before we had met a potential husband!)

But somehow I have accumulated a house, a garage, and a massive shed all full of useless items. And now I must spend my days deciding if any of it sparks bloody joy or not?

But it does work for some people. Check out The Life-Changing Magic of Tidying Up by Marie Kondo.

Some junk accumulation is unavoidable, if you run your own business, for example. You are required to keep 7 years' worth of records. Living in a muddle, surrounded by too much stuff, is bad for your mental wellbeing. This section of the book aims to help you tackle this problem.

I once inherited a house full of antique furniture from an aunt. I admired her and highly valued her opinion. While there were a few pieces I genuinely loved, there were also many items I had no use for. Nor did I have the space to accommodate it all.

Yet I crammed it all in. Filling every nook and cranny in my small house so I could ensure it would all come with me when we moved to a much larger house. We could only use one half of the sitting room because this furniture, which did not fit in anywhere, filled the other half.

Why did I do that?

Mainly because I felt obliged to keep it because she left it to me. As though getting rid of it would be ungrateful and she would have thought badly of me for doing so.

Don't ask! Seems like madness when I think about it now! We all have this inbuilt sense of obligation to things that do not serve us well.

Here are a few more examples:

- Books we started reading but never finished.

- Clothes that may have cost a lot of money, but we don't like. Even though we never wear them, we feel we must keep them.

- Club or gym memberships that we do not enjoy attending anymore.

- People in our lives who make us feel bad when we see or interact with them, but because we have been friends for years, we feel obliged to stay in contact with them.

There is something else too. Something that can cause very distressing thoughts. The promises we make to ourselves about things we do not want to do but say we will, because we get caught up in the moment.

A few months ago, I nearly agreed to run a half marathon! I was watching a friend take part and the friend who was watching with me tried to persuade me to sign up. Thankfully, I stopped myself. I hate running and I knew what would have happened if I had agreed to it.

First, I would have been doing it because somebody else wanted me to do it; not because it was what I wanted to do. This is not a good reason to agree to anything.

Second, my reason to do it would have been to please the other person, not myself. I lacked passion for the run, and I know I would not have committed to any of the training needed.

I would have made excuses and probably would have invented an injury or some other reason not to do it. Potentially, this would have really annoyed my friend; I would have been letting her down and it may even have damaged our friendship. On top of all that, I would have had a nagging, guilty feeling that I should be training.

When you commit to something that deep down inside you know you do not want to do, it can make you feel anxious

Take my advice

Hints and Tips to clear some space

If you are reading a book and you are not enjoying it, or it feels like a punishment to read it; put it aside or give it away.

Clothes -Ask yourself these questions:

- When was the last time you wore an item? If ever. Why don't you wear it?

- Does it fit you? – No? Then do you love it enough that you are prepared to lose gain/weight for it to fit? No? Then let it go. Does it fit you? – Yes! Put in the maybe pile.

- Do you have to twist and turn and pose in the mirror to feel good in it when you put it on? – Yes? Then you will probably never feel comfortable in it. It must go.

- Does it make you feel good? No? Say thank you and goodbye.

- What sort of occasion would you wear it to? Do you have this kind of occasion coming up soon? No? Let it go. Yes? – keep it for that, but if you choose not to wear it, time for it to go.

- Are you keeping something for purely sentimental reasons? Fine, keep it if you have the space.

- Take unwanted clothes to the charity shop, give them away or sell them on sale sites like Vinted if you have the time to list them and post them. This process can be time consuming.

Memberships of any kind; Ask yourself why you are not using it. Does it still serve you? Do you have the time? If not, ask yourself if you are prepared to make time for this activity? If the answer is no, why not? If you decide the membership really does not serve you, then cancel it or if that is not possible, let it expire. Accept that you made a mistake, or circumstances have changed, and you no longer need it. Let the guilty feeling go. Important: Remember to cancel any payment arrangements for subscriptions, as they are often set to auto-renew.

People. This is the hardest one. Especially if you have known them for a long time or if they are a family member. My rule is, if being in their presence makes me feel bad about myself for any reason, I need to limit the time spent with them or choose to bless and release them from my life.

Summary

So many things seem to make us feel overwhelmed, especially the unexpected. Until recently, I was on a roll and determined to complete this book by the end of May 2024. Then sadly my father-in-law became seriously ill and died at the ripe old age of 87. So, once again, I put the book on the back burner.

This time I took my own advice and instead of constantly focusing on the fact that I wasn't in the right flow/head space to finish the book by the deadline I had imposed, I reminded myself that goals get set in cement, but timings are in sand. Instead of stressing about what I could not do, I made a conscious decision to park it, fully knowing that the time would come when I could dedicate my time to finally completing the book.

This meant that I could devote myself to supporting my husband and the family through a tough time, without feeling resentful or guilty about it. I would love to tell you how to avoid overwhelm completely, but we cannot control every aspect of our lives. All we can do is minimise the disruption that it causes in our lives.

Final advice

Find what is causing your Head Fizzle.

Remember, it is good to have a reset day when you feel overwhelmed.

Don't let one bad day take you off course – accept that it's normal to have good days and bad days.

Taking action is the best way to get your mojo back; don't sit back waiting for it to arrive.

It is ok to say no! Especially when you are only saying yes to please somebody else.

Tell yourself you are excited rather than fearful when experiencing fear.

This is big; Let go of the stuff that no longer serves you, whether it be possessions or other people's opinions of you.

> *'Other people's opinions of you are none of your business.'* - Eleanor Roosevelt

Chapter Nine

Resilience to Brilliance

Resilience comes in many forms.

I am a resilient person, and I have bounced back from many traumatic events throughout my life. Yet writing this chapter has been a bit of a struggle. I am finding it hard to express what I feel in writing.

Life is a continuous journey of ups, downs, and everything in between. We have good times, bad times, and amazing times, but there is also a lot of what I call 'treading water' time, where life just seems to plod along uneventfully.

I believe that resilience is a navigation tool for all these challenges.

There are many components to becoming resilient.

One common misconception we have is that when such-and-such an event happens, everything will be ok. For instance, when I move to a larger house, I will be:

- better organised
- able to cook and clean
- have a better life

Or When I lose weight, I will be:

- much happier
- my life will be perfect

While these changes may make a difference, we need to remember that life is not static. Do you know anyone that genuinely lives a life that is 100% perfect? I don't!

'Enjoy the journey of life and not just the endgame.' –Benedict Cumberbatch.

I often say that life is a journey, and I frequently use the phrase 'enjoy the journey' related to goal setting, where the end result serves as a carrot to guide us towards our desired outcome. However, in this context, I am referring to our actual life journey, where the goal is not to hasten towards our final destination -death, but to savour as much of our life's experiences as possible.

Sometimes our life feels perfect, and at other times it feels like a disaster. Most of the time, we are muddling through. Throughout it all, we are a beautiful work in progress. Once we accept this, we are more likely to feel at peace with ourselves.

Resilience is a key skill that we all possess, one that we all need. But are we all aware of it?

Relish being in the discomfort zone by allowing yourself to make mistakes and learn from the experience.

'The greatest mistake you can make in life is to be continually fearing you will make one.' -Elbert Hubbard

I see many people going through their lives without ever reaching their full potential. They shy away from new experiences or hold back from starting a new career because they are too scared of making a mistake.

As I mentioned in the previous chapter, our brain likes to keep us safe, so mistakenly sends us the message that safety lies in the familiar, when in truth the opposite is true. Think of the times when you really wanted to try something new but were so scared of getting it wrong and looking foolish that you did not try it at all.

How did you feel afterwards? I bet it was not a good feeling.

Recently, I have been through what I am now calling a hibernation period; after going through the horrible experience of losing our business for reasons beyond our control.

I opted out of as many things as possible, focusing on the bare minimum; cooking, cleaning, and looking after the grandchildren. Even continuing to write this book felt impossible, as it made me feel uncomfortable.

But here's the thing. Staying with safe and comfortable has the opposite effect of keeping us feeling safe and happy. When you avoid doing something that scares you. – it plays on your mind and gives you a huge dose of head fizzle.

One of the key features in building resilience is overcoming the fear of failure and doing the things that make us feel uncomfortable and scared (within reason, we don't need to put our lives at risk).

'Everything is difficult before it's easy. Everything is uncomfortable before it's comfortable.' – Hal Elrod

Irrespective of whether you do the things you are afraid of or not, you will still feel the fear.

You will feel so much better once you have faced that fear and done the thing that makes you feel uncomfortable, regardless of whether you succeed or fail. And it is much better for your mental fitness than not facing it at all.

People who face their fears are more likely to recover from setbacks and challenges in the future because they are used to dealing with failure.

Think of it like this; doing regular exercise strengthens the body. Getting into your discomfort zone strengthens the mind.

Recovering from a traumatic event

Full recovery from any setback or trauma rarely happens overnight. We plough through periods of hardship, expecting that one day it will be ok, and we will wake up healed. This roller-coaster of emotions often seems like one step forward and two steps back. If it is a massive life-changing event, there will always be echoes of it in your subconscious.

> *I was not sure if I was going to share this, but here goes.*
> *– Julie*

At 46 years old, I found myself widowed. My husband, under the influence of alcohol, had fallen in the street and hit his head on the kerb. This resulted in massive head trauma exacerbated by a previous injury, resulting in his death.

Apparently, this kind of accident is not an uncommon occurrence. When the police knocked on my door to deliver the bad news, he was still alive, and I called my friend who was also my neighbour to take me to the hospital. By the time she pulled into my drive, I had been told of his passing.

I told her that Phil had died, and her next words shocked me.

'He's not dead, don't be so dramatic,' and 'You can't tell the kids.'

Before you judge her, understand that she spoke the words in shock and disbelief. She did not want it to be true. Now I look back on it with humour. Reflecting on the funny things people say in dire circumstances.

One of the worse things I have ever experienced in my life was telling my children, then aged nineteen and fourteen, that their father had died.

Initially, the police did not know what had happened to him and I experienced one of the scariest hours of my life while they questioned me. They even asked me about the car on my drive with a smashed in front. It was only later in the day that I realised where their line of questioning was going! Thankfully, the pub had caught it all on CCTV, so the police left.

On the first day, my emotions were disbelief and shock. I genuinely believed that I would go to visit him in hospital and have a conversation with him about what had happened.

After that, the first few weeks passed in a haze; with a total lack of sleep. Somehow, with the support of friends and copious amounts of caffeine, I arranged for a funeral. If I did snatch a few moments of sleep, Phil's death was the first thing on my mind when I woke.

If you had known me back then, looking in from the outside, you would have judged that I was coping well. The feeling that life was too short, and that I was going to make the most of it, manifested a manic energy in me.

I was just making the best of it, trying to distract myself while I came to terms with my loss. It was always there, hovering at the back of my mind. Looking back now, I know that the two years after Phil's death were a blur, and I made some unbelievably bad decisions whilst I was feeling vulnerable.

I learned a lot from that experience. I realised I was healing when one morning I discovered it was 10am and I had not thought about Phil's death once since waking up.

Take my advice

Healing from a trauma does not happen overnight. It is an ongoing process of good days, bad days, terrible days, and better days.

Everyone handles life-changing events differently.

There is no blueprint for how you should behave, how you should feel, or how long it takes to heal.

Take each day one at a time. Or even hour by hour, minute by minute, whatever works for you.

They say time is a great healer; that does not mean that you will get over it, more that you will adapt to living with it.

Be kind and patient with yourself.

Focus on living in the present moment.

Sometimes you may feel that you are healing, then you will have a bad day. Recognise that this is part of the process! You are still moving forward.

Believe that you will get through this, and life will improve. As my mother used to say. "It will all be alright in the end."

Seek help when you need it. There is no shame in getting professional help.

It felt right at the time

We often look at past events with regret, sometimes with guilt. When our lives are not how we thought they would be, we may reflect on other times in our past when we made wrong decisions. Or when things did not turn out as we expected.

Here's how I look at this. I based the decision on the circumstances and my knowledge and feelings at that moment in time. While it may have turned out to be a terrible decision, there is no point beating myself up and wallowing in past regrets and mistakes. We are human, and sometimes the best way to learn is the hard way.

It is OK to reflect on what you learned from that experience and apply it to your current situation. But there is no point constantly looking back with regret.

Occasionally we feel a mild embarrassment about something that has happened. It might be something trivial that we have said or done (waking up with a massive hangover and an attack of the 'beer-fear' springs to mind here). But it is amazing how even a small thought can cause huge anxiety. It escalates exponentially as we replay it in our heads repeatedly.

This is where I find the three-day rule comes into play. I tell myself that in 3 days it won't feel nearly as bad as it does right now; in fact, I probably won't ever think about it again!

Adapting to change

Most of us dislike change of any kind; even more when it is something we feel is out of our control. We are creatures of habit. I know that even if I shift the furniture in my living room around; it unsettles me until I get used to the new layout. Unexpected change is the one that unsettles us the most. This could be anything from the loss of a loved one, losing your job, or the children leaving home.

Accept the situation as a challenge to be overcome; believe that there is an end in sight and things will improve.

One of the key skills to aid resilience is the ability to adapt to any kind of change; our first instinct is to fight it.

Remember that our brain operates within the rule 'familiar is safe.'

There are three stages to this process. We move from resistance to contemplation before we arrive at acceptance. Mostly, we want things to return to how they were previously, and we are resistant to any change.

We complain loudly to anyone who will listen about how our circumstances were better before and that may be the case. But I am talking about things that are completely out of our control; things that we must learn to accept. No amount of complaining and moaning will make any difference. It only makes the adaptation process even harder.

The next stage is contemplation. Acknowledging that we cannot change a situation and understanding that the change may be beneficial to us allows us to adapt, which leads to acceptance.

Before long, it becomes the new norm in our lives in the same way that learning a new skill seems difficult when you start out. But which, once you have mastered it, becomes automatic and part of our subconscious.

'What doesn't kill you makes you stronger.'

Another way to develop resilience is to overcome the obstacles we encounter along the way.

Back when I was running my hairdressing salon, things became hard for a while. My husband's business was experiencing some financial difficulties, and the costs of running my business were rising exponentially. I had problems recruiting the right staff; I was working lots more hours to pay for childcare, which in retrospect seems like madness. My only auntie was dying from cancer, and I was experiencing symptoms of an underactive thyroid.

I had a lot on my plate, and all of that on top of looking after my family.

I remember one of my clients telling me about how hard her wealthy daughter was finding life. Even though she was in the envious position of not needing to work. She even had a nanny. I confess I found it extremely difficult not to say something derogatory in response.

I was extremely stressed and focussed solely on my problems. I wasn't sleeping and all I could think about was what was going wrong. This was giving me a major head fizzle. I could not see an end in sight. Thankfully, the salon lease was up for renewal, and I decided it was time to close the business. This meant I could spend more time with my children.

Then my aunt died and left me an inheritance, which gave me a bit of breathing space to change my life and address the other issues.

The funny thing is that a year later, I had a slight problem; so small that I cannot even remember what it was. Yet there I was, feeling the same amount of stress and anguish that I had experienced during that tough period when my problems were much more serious. There was no comparison between the two situations, but they felt the same!

I gave myself a talking to and thought back to the incident with my wealthy client. This experience showed me that all problems are relative. They can be as big or as small as you make them.

The biggest lesson this taught me was that when we encounter these types of situations, we need to focus on the solution rather than the problem.

Take my Advice

If you can't change it, let it go. Try not to think about it.

Complaining about any situation only makes it worse and attracts more of the same. It also drains your energy and that of other people around you.

All problems are relative. Try to put them in perspective. Paul McGee, the sumo guy, has some brilliant advice on this. He asks;

on a scale of 1-10 where 10 = death, where is the current problem? I find this very to be effective.

Focus on how you can change or positively influence the situation, decide what your first steps will be, and implement them as soon as possible.

Tell yourself that this is only a temporary situation. You are going to overcome it and the end is in sight.

Focus on the best possible outcome.

Avoid making major decisions when you are in a low mood.

Limbo

I have faced a few scary situations during my life. Were they scary? Or was it just my perception of the circumstances?

One of the most unsettling situations you can find yourself in is being stuck 'in limbo.'

The dictionary definition for limbo in this context reads:

'The feeling that you are stuck in an uncertain situation that you cannot control and in which there is no progress or improvement'.

This brings with it a horrible feeling of insecurity and fear of the unknown. When we find ourselves in limbo, our mind has a tendency to go into overdrive. We find ourselves stuck in fear mode, imagining all the worst possible outcomes rather than focusing on a positive conclusion.

Recently I found myself in exactly this kind of situation. We experienced a hostile takeover of the premises our business was operating from. We found ourselves with no option other than to put our company into liquidation. I completed the paperwork and then it was a waiting game until the creditors' meeting.

I was living in a state of turmoil and fear and, to make matters worse, the people who had bought our building were extremely nasty to deal with, making veiled threats about what would happen if we did not comply with their demands.

My imagination went into overdrive. Constantly running through many terrible scenarios that would not and did not happen. This situation affected me worse than the loss of my first husband. With Phil's death, I knew what I was dealing with, whereas this was a situation I never expected to encounter. One that I had no control over.

I was physically shaking for weeks. In addition, I was angry with myself for not being able to control my feelings as I had in the past.

Even when the worst was over, I was still suffering. I now realise I was experiencing PTSD.

That year was one of the most challenging I have ever faced, and a massive learning curve for me. Only now, over a year later, am I beginning to feel myself again. I am choosing to focus on the positives.

And you know what? Despite all the misery and fear of that terrible situation, there were also many good things that happened.

Remember, life is a balancing act.

I will never forget the lessons this experience taught me. The main thing I learned is that healing is a day-by-day process. When bad things happen, be kind to yourself.

Other examples of limbo

- Waiting for the results of an interview or an appraisal.

- Your boss has called you to a meeting later and you are not sure if it is for a pat on the back or a reprimand.

- Waiting for a response from your bank about the loan.

- Waiting for a response to anything when you are not sure of the outcome.

I have a mood maker display in my office with lots of quotes which I change regularly, depending on my current mood. The quote I return to most often is the one that says,

'Success is getting up one more time than I fall.'

That is the way I perceive resilience.

Life happens; there are good days and bad. It is our ability to bounce back from the bad days that will strengthen us and help us recover.

Resilience is our ability to see beyond a situation and realise that things will get better; we will survive whatever life throws at us.

Having a resilient mindset is better for your general health and your mental health, too.

Accept and embrace the times when things don't live up to your expectations

It is easy to feel let down and disappointed when things don't match our expectations. It may only be little things.

- You were looking forward to a party, and it turned out it was not as good as you had expected.

- You booked a holiday with the promise of a sea view, but all you can see are the mountains.

Or bigger things.

- You planned to be with your partner for eternity and they left you.

- Your children are not following the life path that you had planned for them.

When we make plans that include other people and outside influences, we cannot always guarantee the outcome. Our journey through life does not follow a straight line; we often stray away from the main path.

When this happens, the easiest way to cope is to embrace the different circumstance rather than fight against it and complain that it has not matched your expectation. Let go of the old vison you had and focus on what is good about the present situation you find yourself in.

Different does not always mean it will be better or that it will be worse

Fear of change; fear of the unknown; fear of unexpected changes in our life circumstances.

If we have no previous experience of the situation we find ourselves in, it is incredibly difficult to cope. Slipping into limbo mode is the easy option.

We need to learn that because we find ourselves in a different place than the one we expected to be in does not mean that it will be worse than the one we were in previously.

We humans are way better at adapting to change than we think we are.

Focus on getting through it, rather than getting over it. Any big event or life change will leave a scar.

The good news is that scars eventually fade, becoming less noticeable as time passes.

People often say that time is a great healer. From my experience, I know this to be true. Self-help and previous knowledge of your past resilience will help speed up this process.

There are some things that you may never get over, losing a loved one, for instance. But you will learn to adjust to the situation without them if you let yourself do so.

Look after yourself – the importance of self-care

When we experience drama or life-changing events, it is very easy to neglect ourselves. We put all our focus on the current event. We may even use the event as an excuse to fall into bad habits.

As an ex-smoker, I still remember occasions when I started smoking again, when faced with a minor problem. There are a couple of unhelpful ways we can react when we experience a life-changing event.

- If it is something we can change, then we may focus so hard on changing the outcome that everything else falls by the wayside.

- If it is a situation where we need to grieve or adjust to a major event, then we may find ourselves in hibernation mode; unable to function. When this happens, we often get in our own way.

Neither of these reactions is that helpful.

Go through the motions - Motion creates momentum

One of the best ways I have found to help build resilience is to just go through the motions.

This is exactly how I got back into writing.

I had this belief; before I even attempted to get back to writing, I had to be full of ideas and enthusiasm. I was constantly craving that feeling of being in flow and continually made excuses for myself. I was feeling very anxious about writing and completing this book. At one point, I seriously considered abandoning it completely.

Thankfully, two things happened that helped me get back into the habit of writing again.

The first thing happened while I was having coffee with my good friend, Cindy. As usual, I was being extremely hard on myself.

'I have nothing to offer anyone,' I whinged.

She made me look around the café and spoke.

'Look around you Julie, how many people in this room do you think have written a book? You have already written over forty thousand words! That is something to be proud of.'

Ooh! I am having a limbic moment just reliving that.

Then I had a call from Penny, my book coach, who reminded me firmly that I had something important to say. She told me how much she had enjoyed editing the chapters that I had sent her so far, and that I must finish it.

I am extremely grateful to these two lovely ladies who gave me the confidence boost that I needed. I would love to say that I applied myself to the task with gusto. And that I was once again in full flow. But that is not the case. I still was fearful of writing, and I was not brimming with ideas like I had been in the past.

Their belief in me gave me the kick I needed to try. And that is exactly how I started. Instead of waiting for the enthusiasm to kick in, I decided I would get into the habit of getting words on paper and worry about the quality of the content later. The Mojo bird was not just going to land on my shoulder and create the momentum I needed to start the process. With luck, the enthusiasm would eventually follow.

There is no better feeling than the one you get when work that has been a struggle, turns into a joy and you cannot wait to get going.

I have just stumbled on a video I made when back when I was just beginning to feel better. It's all about the progress 'from shit to shine! It made me smile. – Julie

Take my advice

Don't wait until you feel in the right frame of mind. Create momentum to activate your mojo.

Live in the moment as much as possible. Lao-Tzu says, "Living in the past creates depression. Living in the future can cause anxiety. Living in the present gives you peace."

Have an attitude of gratitude. I cannot stress this too many times. Find even the smallest things to be grateful about.

Take the first step, without expectation. Go through the motions and focus on one task at a time.

Mental toughness; Exercise your mind and your body

One of the most effective ways to become a resilient person is to train yourself in advance so that you have an endurance mentality. There are many ways to do this.

One way is to become physically strong. You can achieve this by pushing yourself a little harder each time you do something physical. I am not suggesting that you need to become an exercise maniac and spend countless hours in the gym.

Although that is a great way to develop endurance, I believe we are all capable of doing a bit more that we think we can.

For example, when you go for a walk, up the pace slightly each time or challenge yourself to walk for 5 minutes more when you are feeling tired. Or do five more reps in the gym. It is all about pushing yourself a little harder.

It could be as simple as doing the washing up at before bed when you are not feeling the inclination or do not feel you have the energy to do it.

Simple things like this all help to flex the bounce back reflex.

Last word

I like to remind myself that so far my track record for getting through bad days is 100%!

That is pretty good going.

Chapter Ten

Rule Book Roulette

This chapter did not exist in my original plan for this book.

It started as a light-hearted collection of funny observations from my people watching activities over the years. But writing it revealed a deeper purpose. I hope reading helps you find humour in everyday situations that might otherwise feel stressful. Taking the pressure off those human interactions we all face from time to time.

Recently, following conversations with several of my coaching clients, I have reached the conclusion that each of us operates from a unique set of unwritten rules that determine our individual boundaries and values.

Our personal rulebook is a complex creation, shaped heavily by the lessons learned during our upbringing. It contains many weird and wonderful rules, some of which are completely nonsensical! But which can often restrict us in our daily life.

Now and then you may run across someone whose rule book mirrors yours, but this does not happen often.

What if your rules differ completely from the person you are dealing with?

Well, this is where things have can go badly wrong.

The idea for this chapter came when I was waiting patiently in line at a pumpkin patch, of all places!

I was queuing with my grandchildren, and people kept pushing in front of me. I thought to myself, 'Why do I constantly find myself in this same situation?'

That's when it occurred to me that lots of the people I meet are not following the same rules as me.

I operate from the rule *'Wait your turn'* while other people are operating from the rule *'Push ahead and get served first'*, with no regard for anyone else.

Why is this relevant to living a more peaceful life?

How much time do we waste getting angry when people do not comply with the rules we believe are the proper set of rules for life?

Or fuming and getting annoyed when someone crosses some arbitrary line we have created in our head?

By looking at this objectively and accepting that they may be operating from a different rule book to me, I have become more tolerant and less angry in certain situations.

This does not mean I am a pushover and will always respect their set of rules. But now I approach it from a different stance. I have learned to give other people the benefit of doubt.

Now I have started this, my RAS is well and truly activated on this subject!

I constantly encounter situations where someone's rule book differs from mine, sometimes slightly, and sometimes completely.

Let's explore some of these unwritten rules. I bet you can add a few of your own to the list!

Please email info@julie-monks.co.uk with your examples.

At the dinner table

I was an only child, and we had plenty of food to go round. Until I started school, mealtimes were calm, with no competition from siblings. When I started having school dinners, I noticed that children who came from large families seemed to grab as much food as they could, as fast as they could, and then devoured it quickly. My friend, one of 9 children, told me that if she did not consume her food quickly, then one of her siblings was likely to steal it from her plate.

She coped better than I did because I operated from the rule *'Food is plentiful and what is served on my plate is all mine'*. Whereas she was operating from the rule *'Food is scarce, and the competition is fierce'*.

Being Inclusive v Exclusive

Another example that comes from being an only child with no siblings. Growing up, I did not believe I was popular, so I often felt as though I was being excluded. I felt like an outsider. Hence, I adopted the rule, *'Don't leave people out; be inclusive wherever and whenever possible'.*

This means I always chat to people who seem to be on their own and try to include them in a group. For example, mums at the school gate. To me, there is nothing worse than being excluded.

This would be lovely if everyone operates from my rule of *'be inclusive'*, but they don't. They may be operating from the *'Keep your circle tight and don't invite outsiders in'* rule.

Make the first move in conversation v Wait for the other person to instigate.

Lots of my generation grew up with the rule *'Don't speak until you are spoken to.'* This makes it hard for them to open a conversation. If you are operating from the rule, *'Take the initiative and open a conversation'* you will find these people rude.

I am a chatterbox. Personally, I operate on the *'make conversation'* rule. I frequently encounter what I think of as incredibly rude rebuffs. I realise now that they respond in that way because they are in shock! They are operating from the *'Don't speak to strangers'* rule, so are not expecting a random stranger to start a conversation with them.

My *'chat with everyone and anyone'* rule served me very well during my time in direct sales.

Teamwork doesn't always make the dream work

Many people are great collaborators and happy to follow the *'Work as a team'* rule, accepting praise and/or criticism as a team. Others are more likely to seek personal glory and cannot bear to share their ideas or the glory with others.

There is no right or wrong here. It is just the way we like to behave.

Being courteous v Lack of consideration for others

There have been many occasions when I have held a door open for somebody and they have sailed through without acknowledging me, let alone saying 'Thank you'. Because I always make a point of saying thanks, I find it hard to understand this lack of a gracious response and struggle to understand which set of rules they are operating on.

I am the person who says 'Thank You' in a loud and slightly sarcastic voice! Better than slamming the door in their face, I guess.

Speak your mind v Keep your counsel to yourself

Oh, this is a dark area. I grew up with the *'Say what you think, thrash it out and make up afterwards rule'*. Which allows you to have a difference of opinion and fight about it, without falling out indefinitely.

This is all very well, until you find yourself in conflict with a person who is labouring under the non-confrontation rule, *'Don't upset others, even if they have upset you.'*

If this happens, they may take offence and never speak to you again.

These people are probably also working under the influence of the *'Take offence'* program rather than the *'Take advice'* rule.

Kiss and make up v Enemies for life

Speaking of arguments...

Many of us operate with the *'Kiss and make up rule'*.

I see most arguments as a difference of opinion. It's possible to resolve them or reach a compromise. Failing that, the parties involved can simply agree that they have a different opinion and leave it at that.

Other people feel a need to get the other person to agree with them. If they fail, they will make that person an enemy for life.

If this happens, try not to take it personally. They are just operating from *the 'Hold a grudge'* rule, the opposite of your *'Let's all be friends again'* rule.

Gossip

Some groups of people seem to thrive on gossiping about others and finding fault, whereas others operate from the *'It's rude to talk about another person behind their back'* rule.

Some people love to give and receive compliments, while others thrive on criticising others.

I find it interesting to observe all the different rulebooks in action. When we see that some of our rules are not working for us, it can make a massive difference.

For example, I used to have a terrible habit; always looking for flaws in people and focusing on the bad things about them.

Now I have changed my operating system to *'Always look for the best in other people'*. Boy! What a positive difference this has made in my life!

Rather than operating from the rule of *'Judgment'*, I try to embrace the *'Keep an open mind'* rule.

Keeping other secrets

This can be a tough one. If someone tells you something in confidence, you should never ever discuss it with anyone else. Or should you? This is a bit of a grey area.

Let's say someone has told you something that, if not shared, could be detrimental to them for their own health or safety. If this is the case, then there is a time and a place to break that rule.

Go the extra mile v Do the bare minimum

At work, you may work with a person whose mantra is *'Do the bare minimum'* while you operate from the *'Go the extra mile'* program. This leads to frustration on both sides and can cause resentment.

Solution focused v Problem focused

One person is programmed to *'Look for a solution to every problem'*, whilst another is running on *'Focus and worry about the problem'*.

This causes frustration; you want to vent about a problem to get it off your chest while the other person is coming up with solutions left, right and centre. While you, at that point in time, have no intention of addressing the problem.

Calm v Dramatic in a crisis

Some people positively thrive in a crisis, taking charge while others panic and cannot take control.

There are people who will see even the smallest problem as an enormous mountain to climb and turn it into an equally huge drama. While a person operating on the *'All problems are here to be tackled and overcome'* rule remains calm and collected, no matter how big the problem appears.

Savers v Spenders

This one causes a lot of arguments. (see Chapter 6 Money).

Growing up, I lived in an environment of scarcity and save. This means I always think about what I am spending, only spend what I have and always have a budget.

When I encounter people with a *'spend now and worry about the consequences later'* attitude, it makes me feel uncomfortable and anxious.

Generous v Selfish

One person may take great pleasure in being generous and doing things to help other people. Another person will always put themselves first.

This is one rule that often causes discord or arguments. For instance, when a group of you are eating out and it comes to splitting the bill. The generous spenders among the group are happy to split the bill equally, whereas the savers and the ones with the meagre mindset will query every item on the bill and only want to pay for exactly what they had. 'I didn't have dessert!'

Organised v Chaotic

This often causes massive arguments, especially in the workplace. One person is methodical and businesslike; they run their life with military precision. But another likes to fly by the seat of their pants and is completely happy to exist in disorganised chaos.

This pairing works well when a person who likes to take control of a situation is paired with someone who loves to let others take control.

However, this is a recipe for disaster if you have two control freaks who both want to be in charge. It is also not great when a there are no leaders in a group.

Shows v Hides emotions to/from others

Some people are open books or over-sharers when it comes to showing their feelings and emotions in public. Others operate from the *'stiff upper lip'* rule and hate public displays of emotion.

Self-conscious v Self confident

'Dance as though no one is watching' versus *'Oh, I couldn't get up in front of people and have them looking at me!'*

Punctual v late

There are so many variations to this rule!

Jane operates on the *'Always be dead on time'* rule, whereas Jackie runs on the *'Always arrive early'* program.

While Jeanette is operating on the *'10 minutes late counts as on time'* rule, Jasmine is running on the *'Well, I am always late, everybody expects if of me'* rule.

As I operate from the Jackie rule, I find it extremely frustrating when encountering anyone on the Jeanette and Jasmine programs.

What is important to you is not always important to others

We need to understand that everyone has a unique set of priorities. This influences the rules from which we operate. What may be of high importance to us is of little significance to another.

Once we understand this, we can live a much more harmonious life.

To help you gain a deeper understanding of how all this works, try reading 'The 5 love languages' By Gary Chapman

When I first got together with my husband, we would occasionally have a row. It used to drive me mad when he would simply walk away in the middle of it.

My previous husband would just retreat into silent mode when I shouted at him. All that did was make me angrier.

This might explain why I have been married 3 times! I sound like an extremely angry wife, don't I?

We all have different ways of reacting to an argument.

We can choose from fight, flight, or fright.

It's easy to guess my go to! I always choose fight.

Husband no 2 was operating from fright; he grew up with parents that rarely argued in his presence, so he would opt for silence.

Husband no 3 opts for flight as he does not like confrontation. This helped me understand why he reacts the way he does. I have learned that if he exits the room; it is not a good idea to run after him, shouting. He is removing himself and will come back when the situation has calmed down.

Just in case you are wondering what category husband no 1 came under. Dear Reader, I am afraid that I was very young and idealistic all those years ago and did not stay with him long enough to find out! I must have been operating from the flight rule back then.

Summary

This chapter has taken me much longer to write than I thought it would.

Having explored the subject, I am amazed by how many different sets of rules I come across every day! It reminded me again of the book, The 7 Habits of Highly effective people by Stephen Covey.

Habit #5 states; Seek first to understand, then to be understood.

My main reason for including this chapter is to help you understand that not everyone is following the same rules or running the same program as you. By looking at things from their standpoint and gaining an understanding, we can save ourselves unnecessary anguish and time-wasting thoughts about another person's behaviour when we are interacting with them.

By becoming an observer, we can have a bit of fun with certain situations rather than getting stressed about them.

We humans will never agree on everything. Accepting this and learning to respect each other's rules will make for a happier life all round.

Most of us know that to resolve difficult situations, we need to find a compromise. Knowing that people are all operating with their own set of rules should help us find common ground more quickly and help us feel happier even if we do not always achieve our desired result.

Have yourself some fun observing and implementing your own personal rules for life.

Epilogue

End of Part One!

17th September 2024

Well, here I am, almost at the end, after four...shall we say, interesting years.

Thank goodness for Penny, my friend and amazing book coach. She has helped me in so many ways, from structuring the book and choosing the chapter topics, to invaluable help with spelling and grammar. Like I say in the Taking Action chapter, sometimes you need to pay for professional help.

Yes, I do take my own advice occasionally.

When I started writing this book, we were in the middle of a pandemic. Being confined at home most of the time meant I had plenty of time.

I could never have imagined quite how many life-changing events would happen in the next few years. My mother and my father-in-law passing away. Three more beautiful grandchildren arriving, taking our total to eight. My daughter needing my help after divorcing her husband. And the biggest change of all, losing our structural steel painting business, which changed our lives dramatically.

There have been some amazing highs, but I have also experienced some of the lowest points in my life. These things have all influenced the progression of the book. I feel like a slightly different Julie from the one who started out with a few ideas in my head four years ago.

All these experiences have given me plenty of material to write about and there have definitely been times when I have ignored my own advice, to my detriment. The good news is that I have learned lots of valuable lessons, too.

It's interesting where life's journey takes you. I thought I had semi-retired and yet at 64 here I am starting a new coaching business and feeling full of enthusiasm.

I also have plenty of fodder for another book, too!

Thank you for reading my book. I hope you have enjoyed the ride!

Reading List

Books you might like almost as much as this one!

Here is a selection of the books that have helped and motivated me over the years.

Being Happy - *by Andrew Matthews*

One of the very first personal development books that I read way back in 1998. This taught me to take responsibility for my own life and actions. A great easy read with fab illustrations

How to be Brilliant - *by Michael Heppell*

When you need enthusiasm and inspiration.

Just Fucking Do It - *by Noor Hibbert*

I loved this! It felt like Noor was on my wavelength. This was the book that kicked me up the backside and got me writing the book that I have long been procrastinating about writing.

The 5 Languages of Love - *by Gary Chapman*

A book that explains the way others think and how you can interact with them with understanding. A game-changer.

The 7 Habits of Highly Effective People - *by Stephen R Covey*

This is a classic which I recommend everyone should read. Another one that changed my life in the early days of my direct sales career.

The Secret - *Rhonda Byrne*

A fab introduction to the law of attraction.

The Magic - *Rhonda Byrne*

One of my favourites. It contains an exercise for each day on how to harness the law of attraction. This is one I go back to, time after time.

You are a Badass - *Jen Sincero*

This book is for you if you suffer from imposter syndrome and self-doubt.

Energy Alignment Method – Yvette Taylor

I learned about this method five years ago. This is the book to help you let go of limiting thought beliefs and so much more.

S.U.M.O. Your Relationships (How to handle not Strangle the People you Live and Work With) - *Paul McGee*

I came across Paul in my Virgin cosmetics days. To this day, I still use his 7 questions to use when faced with a challenge.

Eat That Frog – *Brian Tracy*

Another one of my early reads and one to read when you are struggling with overwhelm.

Believe It to Achieve It - *Brian Tracy*

Overcome your doubts and unlock your full potential.

Body Language - *Allan Pease*

An essential recommendation: everyone should read this one. We all underestimate how important reading other people's body language is.

Questions are the Answers - *Allan Pease*

An absolute must if you are in any social selling business. It teaches you to focus on the law of averages, making those sales approaches seem enjoyable.

Do You Have the Time for Success? - *Julio Melara*

This book really inspired me to explore and set goals.

The Miracle Morning - *Hal Elrod*

If you want to get your day off to an amazing start and design a morning routine, this is the one for you.

Ask and it is Given - *Esther & Jerry Hicks*

A nice introduction to the law of attraction with lots of practical exercises, too.

Atomic Habits - *James Clear*

An easy & proven way to build good habits and break bad ones.

Who moved my Cheese - Dr *Spencer Johnson*

A must read when facing any kind of change.

Find Your Why - *Simon Sinek*

For finding your purpose and discovering what motivates you personally.

The Richest Man in Babylon - *George S Clason*

This is one of those that I believe everyone should read. Essential for creating a good relationship with your money.

The Life-Changing Magic of Tidying Up – *Marie Kondo*

If you are at the stage in your life where you are trying to work and run a household, Marie Kondo is the guru. My house has always been tidy and easy to maintain since reading this book.

Do you have a favourite book that has helped you on your journey? I would love to add to my list.

Email me on info@julie-monks.co.uk

Printed in Great Britain
by Amazon